PROPERTY OF WAYNE COUNTY
INTERMEDIATE SCHOOL DISTRICT
CHAPTER 2, P.L. 97-35

GESU SCHOOL LIBRARY
DETROIT, MICH. 48221

VISUAL SCIENCE
METALS

Robin Kerrod

Silver Burdett Company

Editor John Rowlstone
Design Richard Garratt
Consultant Tony Osman
Picture Research Jenny Golden
Production Susan Mead

First published 1981

Macdonald Educational Ltd.
Holywell House
Worship Street
London EC2A 2EN

©Macdonald Educational 1981

Adapted and Published in
the United States by
Silver Burdett Company,
Morristown, New Jersey

1982 Printing

ISBN 0-382-06661-8

Library of Congress
Catalog Card No. 82-50388

Cover: plasma laser cutting through steel
Right: billets of aluminium on dockside

Contents

- 4   The nature of metals
- 6   Uses of metals
- 8   The big three
- 10 Metals and civilization
- 12 Metals under the microscope
- 14 Metal mixtures
- 16 Metals under attack
- 18 Testing and measuring metal
- 20 Sources of metals
- 22 Mining methods
- 24 From mine to metal
- 26 Smelting the ore
- 28 Electrochemical extraction
- 30 Refining methods
- 32 Shaping hot metal
- 34 Shaping cold metal
- 36 Joining and cutting metal
- 38 Machining metal
- 40 Decorative metalwork
- 42 Metals tomorrow
- 44 A-Z glossary
- 46 Reference
- 48 Index

The nature of metals

Below: Chromium is plated on cheaper metals such as steel to protect them from corrosion and to make them look more attractive, for example as car trim.

Right: Printed circuits are a modern-day use for the oldest known metal – copper. Circuits are formed in a copper film by a printing and etching technique.

Above: Cast-iron cooking utensils are used by many cooks because they retain heat well from the cooking source. If properly treated, the surface of the pan becomes virtually 'non-stick'.

Above: Mercury, the only metal that is liquid at ordinary temperatures, is used widely in barometers and thermometers. Mercury freezes at −39°C so it is unsuitable for measuring very low temperatures.

Above: Aluminium has many everyday uses, including window frames and milk bottle-tops. Only a few metals are malleable enough to be able to form a thin film without any structural weakness.

All the matter on our planet, whether it is rocks, air, wood, flesh, diamonds, water, or a television set, is made up of different combinations of basic 'building blocks' called the chemical elements. In turn each element is made up of smaller 'building blocks' called atoms, and each atom consists of a central nucleus surrounded by electrons. A cubic centimetre of copper, for example, contains about 80,000,000,000,000,000,000,000 atoms.

What are metals?

In all, 92 chemical elements are found in Nature. No less than 70 of them are metals. If you looked out of the window it might well seem that metals are hard, tough and very strong shiny substances that are used to build machines and structures like bridges and skyscrapers, and to make all kinds of useful tools and instruments.

Steel and aluminium are certainly like this. But other metals are neither hard, tough nor strong. At ordinary temperatures sodium, for example, is as soft and weak as putty and can easily be cut with a knife, whilst mercury is a liquid. But both sodium and mercury are classed as metals. Lithium, the lightest metal, can even float in water.

Steel, aluminium, sodium and mercury have several things in common with each other and with other metals. They have a shiny surface and they conduct heat and electricity well. These properties as a rule set metals apart from the rest of the chemical elements, collectively termed 'non-metals'.

Half the non-metals are gases; one is a liquid (bromine) and the rest are solids. The solid non-metals are in general dull and do not conduct heat and electricity well. They are good insulators.

Defining a metal by its appearance and conductivity is still not wholly satisfactory, since there are exceptions. One form of the non-metal arsenic, for example, actually looks like a metal, whereas the non-metal carbon can be a good conductor of electricity. So the chemist has a more precise definition of a metal: a chemical element that in solution forms ions with a positive electrical charge. These 'positive ions' are atoms which have lost one or more electrons. The only exception to this rule is the non-metal hydrogen.

Below: Electrical cable is probably the most familiar use of copper because the metal is the best low-cost electrical conductor. It can also be easily drawn into wire.

Right: The jaws of this bulldozer are made from manganese steel, which is exceptionally tough and hard-wearing.

Above: A dry battery is encased in zinc, which takes part in an electrochemical reaction that produces electricity. The connecting terminals are of brass, a copper-zinc alloy.

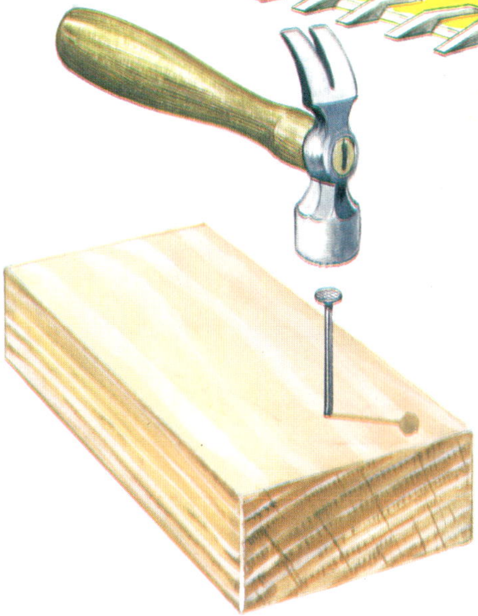

Above: Hammers usually have a head of hardened steel to force nails into wood.

Below: When laying railway lines, engineers must leave gaps between the rails to allow the metal to expand in very hot weather.

Above: Most metals are very much stronger than non-metals. High-rise buildings are made possible by constructing a framework of steel girders.

The chemistry of metals comes into its own in the extraction of a metal from its ore and its resistance to chemical corrosion.

Properties

Like all elements, the metals combine chemically with other elements to form a variety of compounds or alloys. Each individual metal or alloy has its own properties which fit it for some special purpose. These properties largely determine how a metal is used.

Metals that are used in construction need to be particularly strong to support the structural loads. Metals for cutting tools need to be particularly hard so that they keep their cutting edge.

Some metals that are strong and hard, however, are of little use because they snap easily. They are brittle. Brittle metals are very difficult to work with and have only limited uses. Cast iron is probably the most common brittle metal. However, there are many metals that are easy to work with, that can be hammered or rolled into shape (a property called malleability), or stretched a lot without breaking (ductile strength).

Metallurgy

The study of metals is called metallurgy. It covers the science of extracting metals from their ores, preparing them for use, and studying their structure and properties. It is normally divided into ferrous (iron and steel) and non-ferrous metallurgy. The iron and steel industry is one of the world's most important.

5

Uses of metals

Above: Steel is the main material for suspension-bridge construction. A steel deck hangs from steel cables that pass up and over steel towers.

Bronze is a favourite metal for casting statues. It melts readily and flows easily, allowing accurate reproduction of detail.

Aircraft frames are constructed from aluminium alloys because they are both light and strong.

The nuclear submarine is fuelled by uranium. A small amount of this fuel can provide enough power for the vessel to remain for months submerged, without the need to refuel.

In one form or another we use practically all the metals that exist in the Earth's crust. A metal may be selected for a particular use because of its physical properties – strength, hardness, brittleness, malleability, and ductility – or its electrical or chemical properties. Or it may have other individual properties that make it suitable. For example, iron has its magnetism, uranium its radioactivity, and platinum its unrivalled ability as a catalyst.

Alloys

Each pure metal has its own particular set of properties. Few have the right combination to make them suitable for more than one or two applications. But fortunately pure metals can be blended together to give mixtures, or alloys. By carefully selecting the metals for blending, an alloy can usually be obtained that has better properties than any one of the parent metals. That is why most metals are used in the form of alloys.

The illustrations give an indication of the variety of ways we use metals. In bridge construction, for example, steel is the favourite material because it is cheap and strong. Even when concrete is used for bridges, it is strengthened with steel rods. By itself, concrete is

Left: Most cars are made mainly of iron and steel. The body is painted mild steel sheet, while the main engine block is cast iron. Other parts are made of hardened steel alloys. The car has stainless steel or chromium-plated steel trim. Copper is used for the electrical wiring.

Right: Iron is not only valuable for its strength, but also because it is magnetic. Without this property, there would be no electromagnets nor electric motors and generators.

very strong under pressure but weak if stretched. Concrete reinforced with steel rods removes this structural weakness.

Suspension bridges, which can span the biggest gaps, rely on the enormous strength of steel wire. Hundreds of thousands of kilometres of steel wire make up the cables that support the bridge deck. The wire is galvanized, or coated with zinc, to prevent it rusting. Thus the metallurgist has been able to get the best of both worlds – both strength and corrosion resistance.

In aircraft construction weight is very important so designers naturally go for aluminium, the lightest common metal. To make it suitably hard and strong, it is alloyed with a little copper. Rusting, or corrosion, presents no problem because aluminium is naturally covered with a protective film.

Titanium may be selected for parts of high-speed aircraft that experience high temperature. The metal keeps its strength at high temperatures. Nickel, chromium and tungsten are also used in the high-temperature parts of jet and rocket engines.

Titanium is used by the Russians in their latest nuclear submarines, which can travel deeper and faster than any built in the West. The nuclear submarine is powered by a reactor, which works because the metal fuel it contains – uranium – is unstable. Its atoms are continually breaking down, giving off atomic particles and enormous heat.

The heat from this reaction is controlled and used to generate steam for the turbines that drive the propeller.

The propeller incidentally, like most ships' propellers, is cast in aluminium bronze, which is very strong and resists attack by seawater. Ordinary bronze (copper and tin) is a favourite material for casting statues. It is very fluid when molten and can reproduce detail sharply. It also resists attack by the weather quite well.

The metallic car

The ordinary motor car contains as bewildering a variety of different metals and alloys as we are likely to find anywhere. Each of the several hundred car components makes special demands which the metallurgist must meet if the car is not continually to break down.

While the bulk of the car is cast iron (engine block) and mild steel (body), special alloy steels are used for the prop shaft, camshaft, connecting rods, gears and ball bearings. The contact breakers incorporate tungsten; the battery has lead plates which react chemically with dilute sulphuric acid to supply electricity; the generator uses copper and all electric wiring is made of copper; the trim is of stainless steel or chromium plate; and the door handles are of plated zinc alloy.

The list is seemingly unending, as are the number of uses to which metals singly and in combination can be put.

Right: A carpenter's work has been made much easier since metal woodworking tools came into use. Most cutting tools are made from hard carbon steels so that they keep their cutting edge.

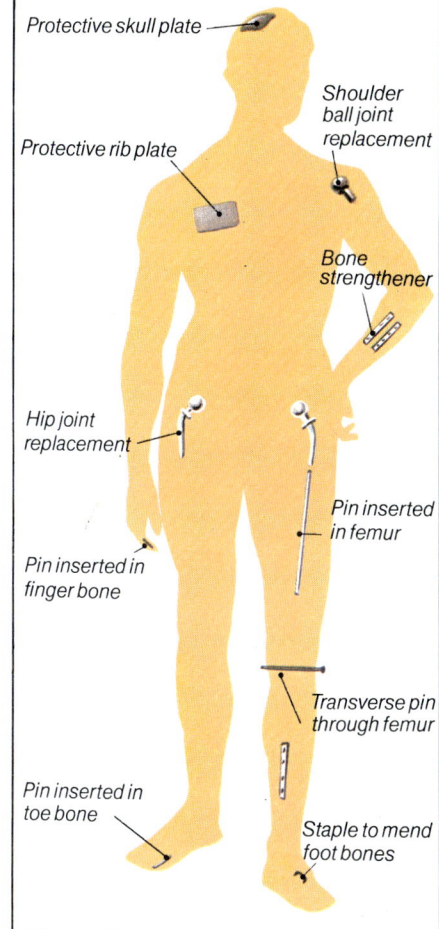

Above: Metals play their part in surgery too. When bones have been badly broken, they can be reinforced with metal plates and pins. Stainless steel, titanium and silver are used because they do not react with body tissues.

Above: Food and drink are packaged in aluminium and tinplate containers which are coated on the inside with lacquer.

Below: The precious metals gold, silver and platinum are widely used in jewellery.

Above: Grinding wheels are made of a tough composite material containing tungsten carbide, which approaches diamond in hardness.

The big three

Three metals stand out above the rest in terms of their usefulness and production tonnage. These are iron, aluminium and copper. Worldwide, more than 600 million tonnes of iron are produced annually. More iron is produced than all of the other metals put together. Aluminium is produced at the rate of only about 11 million tonnes a year. Copper has a production rate of about 6 million tonnes a year.

Iron

Iron is outstanding among metals because it can readily be made into steel. Steel is an alloy, or rather a range of alloys, noted for its great strength. It is the presence of traces of carbon in steels that gives them their unique value. Iron also has the other valuable property of being magnetic.

Iron is one of the most widely available metals there is. There are vast iron-ore deposits worldwide. The Earth's crust contains over 5 per cent of the metal. But it comes out of the ground in the form of minerals, not as a metal. However these minerals, or ores, can be easily converted into metallic iron.

Russia has the world's largest iron mine at Kursk, about 500 kilometres south-west of Moscow. It has reserves estimated at over 10 million million tonnes of iron ore. The region near Magnitogorsk in the Southern Urals, the Lake Superior region in North America, and the Hamersley and Middleback Ranges in Australia also hold large iron reserves.

The most important iron ores, in order of their iron content, are magne-

Above: Copper is valuable not only in its own right, but also because it forms a wide range of alloys. The best-known of these are brass and bronze, each of which have a host of uses. Brass can be shaped by cold working whereas bronze is cast into shape.

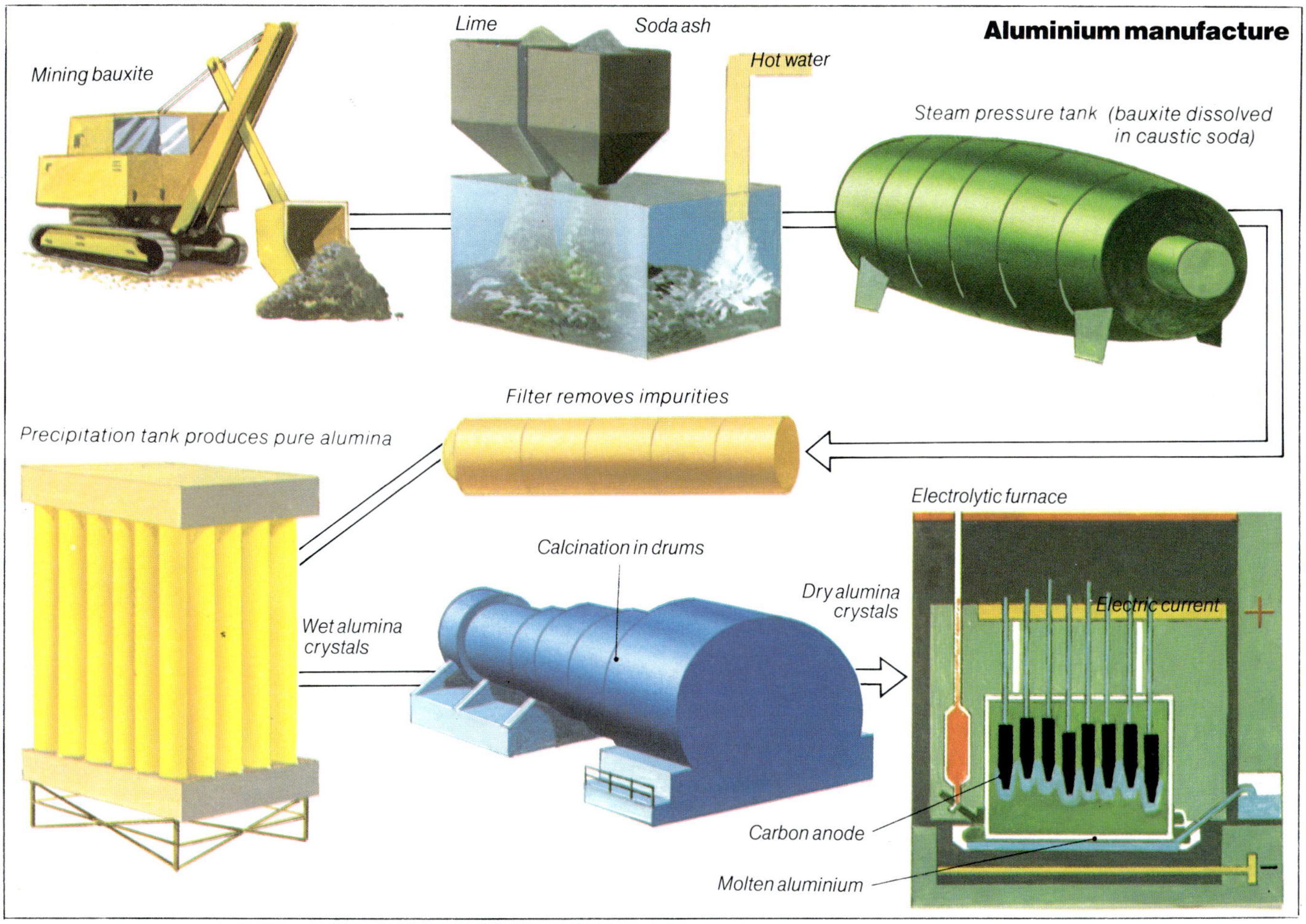

Aluminium manufacture

Mining bauxite — Lime — Soda ash — Hot water — Steam pressure tank (bauxite dissolved in caustic soda) — Filter removes impurities — Precipitation tank produces pure alumina — Wet alumina crystals — Calcination in drums — Dry alumina crystals — Electrolytic furnace — Electric current — Carbon anode — Molten aluminium

tite, haematite, limonite and siderite. Black magnetite, so-called because it is a natural magnet, is iron oxide. Haematite, named because of its blood-red appearance, is also an oxide.

Aluminium

The special property that makes aluminium so useful is its lightness. It has only about one-third of the density of steel, but it can be alloyed to be almost as strong as steel. Aluminium is the best cheap conductor of electricity and heat, hence its use for electricity transmission lines, and pots and pans for cooking. It also resists corrosion well.

The Earth's crust contains even more aluminium than iron, over 8 per cent. It is found in ordinary garden clay, for example, but the only profitable way of obtaining aluminium is from bauxite, an oxide ore.

Bauxite is much scarcer than iron ore and is more expensive to process into metal. Australia has the biggest bauxite deposits, at Weipa in Queensland, and produces 25 per cent of the world's output. Jamaica and Brazil also have vast deposits.

Copper

Copper is highly rated as a metal for several reasons. It is a superb conductor of electricity and heat. It is highly ductile, and can be drawn easily into fine wire. And it resists corrosion well. It also blends well with other metals to form a huge range of very useful alloys.

Copper stands in complete contrast to aluminium, which has been produced in quantity for less than 100 years, because it is probably the oldest metal worked by man. This happened because it was occasionally found as lumps of metal ('native' copper).

There are a number of suitable ores among the 300 or so minerals that contain copper. They include chalcocite (copper sulphide), chalcopyrite (mixed copper and iron sulphides), cuprite (copper oxide), and the carbonates malachite and azurite. Chalcopyrite has the metallic yellow glint of gold, and is well-named 'fool's gold'. Malachite (blue-green) and azurite (azure blue) are two of the most vividly coloured minerals. The 'Copperbelt' of Zimbabwe and Zambia is one of the largest deposits in the world.

Above: The diagram shows the method by which aluminium is extracted and refined from its ore, bauxite. The aluminium oxide (alumina) in the ore is purified by chemical means and then split by electricity into aluminium metal and oxygen.

Below: Iron girders are used in all kinds of engineering projects. These girders are exposed to the wind and rain and are already beginning to show signs of corrosion.

Metals and civilization

Above: Intricate casting by the 'lost wax' process has been practised for over 5,000 years. The famous African 'Benin bronzes' were cast by this method. A model is first shaped roughly in clay. It is then coated in wax and the detail carved on it. A further layer of clay is then put over the wax carving to make a mould. Molten metal is poured into the clay mould and this melts the wax layer, thus reproducing the exact shape in the mould. After cooling, the clay mould is broken away to reveal the casting.

Man has been using metals in one form or another for probably as long as 10,000 years. Metals gave early man better tools and sharper weapons with which he could exercise greater mastery over his environment. And it was man's increasing use of metals that led to the growth of large permanent settlements and our present society's dependence on metals.

Copper and bronze

The first metal man used was probably native copper, lumps of which could occasionally be found on the ground. But it was so scarce that it was at first only used for beads and jewellery. Tools and weapons were still made of stone. Then, in about 5000 BC, people in Egypt and Mesopotamia discovered how to smelt copper from its ores.

Left: The launching in July 1843 of the *Great Britain*, built by Isambard Kingdom Brunel. She was the first large iron-built ship to regularly sail the Atlantic.

By 3500 BC copper was being smelted and cast into tools and utensils throughout the world, except in the Far East and the Americas where a Stone Age still continued.

But the increasingly expert metal-workers then stumbled across an alloy that was to dominate civilization for the next 2,000 years – bronze. Made at first by smelting mixed copper and tin ores, it had the hardness and strength lacked by the earlier metals. Bronze was thus a much better material for making tools and weapons, and it could easily be cast into shape.

Iron Age

Iron was first used in the Eastern Mediterranean region in about 1500 BC. But the Iron Age did not begin in Western Europe and China until some 900 years later.

The early iron smelters produced iron in a spongy form mixed with slag. Their furnaces were not as yet hot enough to melt it. The metalworkers then beat the slag from the iron by repeated hammering, and then hammer-forged it into shape. It was a form of iron that we now call wrought iron. Ironworkers soon discovered that they could harden the iron by heating it in contact with charcoal and then plunging it while red-hot into water. They were in effect making a form of steel and hardening it by quenching.

The Chinese were late in developing the use of iron but were remarkable in being able to cast it almost from the beginning. Elsewhere in the world, cast iron did not become available until iron-smelting furnaces assumed something like their present form in about AD 1400.

Modern metallurgy

The discovery in 1709 that coke could replace charcoal for iron smelting resulted in bigger and hotter furnaces and the movement of metalworking areas closer to coalfields. The cast iron thus produced was mainly converted into wrought iron by 'puddling' furnaces. As industry expanded so did the

Above: The gold funeral mask of Tutankhamun is perhaps the best-known archaeological treasure in the world. It dates from the 14th century BC.

demand for vast quantities of both cast and wrought iron for steam engines, rails, spinning machines, bridges and so on.

After 1856, when Henry Bessemer introduced a process for making it cheaply, steel became the dominant metal. Experiments with different steel mixtures led to the development of alloy steels such as invar, cutting steel and stainless steel.

Perhaps the most remarkable feature of 20th century metallurgy has been the growth in the use of a metal virtually unknown before the 1850s – aluminium. It has only been produced in quantity since 1886, when Charles Hall in the United States and Paul Héroult in France independently invented the modern electrolytic smelting process. Now aluminium is second in importance only to steel.

Metals under the microscope

Mineral specimen

Below: Much of interest can be revealed by examining a metallic mineral ore under a microscope. But it must be carefully prepared. The diagram shows how to prepare a slide for a microscope in order to reveal the crystal structure.

Apart from the fact that they are both solid, diamond and iron would appear to have nothing in common. But they are both composed of crystals. All metals are made up of crystals, although they cannot usually be seen with the naked eye. The crystals do, however, show up under the microscope after the metal surface has been suitably treated. Metallurgists call these metal crystals grains, so this term will be used from now on.

phosphor-bronze cutting wheel

1. The rock specimen is cut using a circular saw, forming a very thin cross-section of the mineral.

Grain structure

The nature and size of the grains in a metal have a great effect on its properties. The grains can be altered by heat, by the presence of 'foreign bodies', such as other metals, and by mechanical treatment, such as forging and rolling. By observing the grain structure of a metal, metallurgists can learn a lot about its behaviour.

2. The slice is suitably mounted on a slide, and one face is polished. This is done by using progressively finer grades of emery cloth and finishing with polishing powder.

One method involves preparing a thin metal specimen for examination under the microscope. It is polished and etched with acid, which attacks the boundaries between the grains. When observed under the microscope, the more deeply etched grain boundaries stand out as dark lines. In the case of metal alloys, the acid attacks the different grains in varying degrees. This also makes the grains stand out.

Slice covered with glass plate ready for microscope

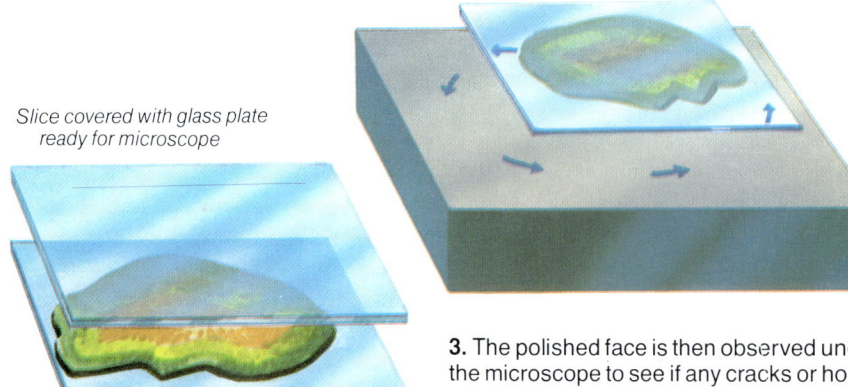

3. The polished face is then observed under the microscope to see if any cracks or holes are present.

Even greater detail of grain structure can be revealed under an electron microscope. This uses a beam of electrons, rather than light, to examine the specimen metal. Whereas the ordinary optical metallurgical microscope magnifies up to about 1000 times, the electron microscope magnifies tens of thousands of times.

4. Further details can be seen after etching (treating the surface with acid). The acid mainly attacks the specimen at the grain boundaries.

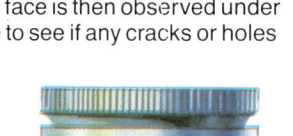

However, no microscope is required to see the grains of zinc on galvanized buckets and baths. In galvanizing, steel is dipped in molten zinc, which forms beautiful and easily visible feathery crystals when it cools.

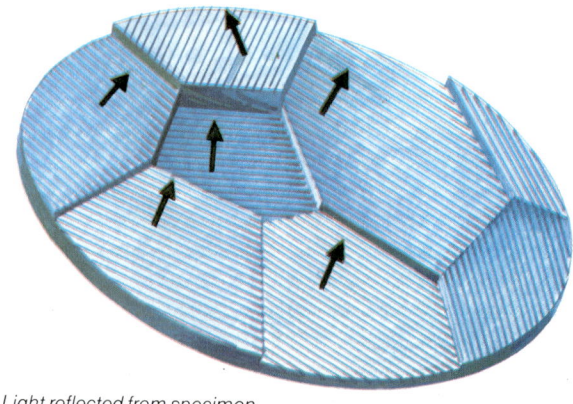

5. When observed under the microscope, the etched grains reflect light in different directions and thus the grain structure becomes visible.

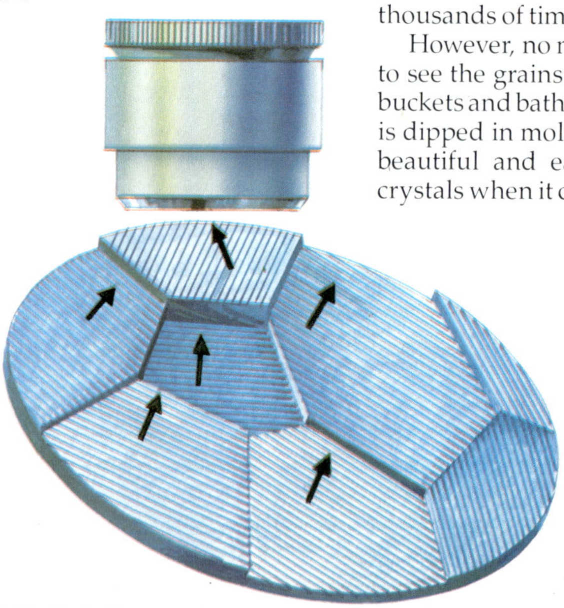

Light reflected from specimen according to effect of etching on different grains

12

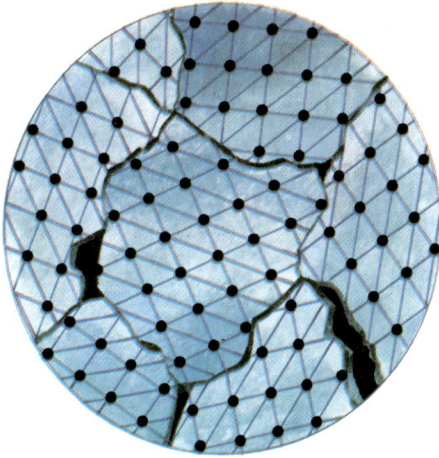

Above: The shape of the crystal lattice varies from one metal to another. A fractured piece of metal under the microscope would look like a row of closely-packed skyscrapers.

Above: The boundaries between the crystals, or grains, show up clearly under a microscope. They look like islands jammed together, but each island is made up of a regular lattice structure of atoms.

Above: Metal crystals grow into a characteristic shape, like a tree with branches and leaves, called a dendrite. It is clearly seen here in the surface of this specimen of antimony.

Crystal lattice

Under the right conditions feathery or tree-like growths can be found in other metals. All metals in fact start to form tree-like formations, or dendrites, when they crystallize from the molten state. The regular shape of a dendrite is a development of the fundamental structure of the metal, the crystal lattice. The lattice is made up of atoms arranged in a certain way, which varies from metal to metal.

In copper, aluminium and gold, for example, the basic lattice consists of a cube with atoms at each corner and in the middle of each face. This arrangement is called face-centred cubic. Sodium, tungsten and iron at room temperatures have a basic lattice that has atoms at the corners of a cube, with a single atom in the cube's centre. This arrangement is called body-centred cubic. Zinc and magnesium have a six-sided, or hexagonal lattice. These three crystal lattices are the most common ones in metals. Iron is interesting in that it changes at high temperatures into a face-centred cubic lattice.

The crystal structure of metals can be investigated by means of X-rays. When a beam of X-rays is fired through a thin metal specimen, it is scattered, or diffracted, in a characteristic pattern. This shows up the atomic structure of the metal.

The lattice structure of a metal is seldom perfect, however. There is usually an irregularity, or dislocation, in the structure due to extra or missing atoms. Dislocations cause weakness and allow planes of atoms to slip and fracture when they are put under stress. Normally, if the lattice remains intact under stress, failure occurs at the grain boundaries.

Below left and **below:** Four different metallic mineral ores are shown here. On the left are ordinary specimens whilst on the right the crystal structure of each ore is shown by magnifying the specimen 30 times. The red ore is haematite (iron), the grey ore is covellite (copper), the pink one is rhodochrosite (manganese), and the green specimen is autunite (uranium).

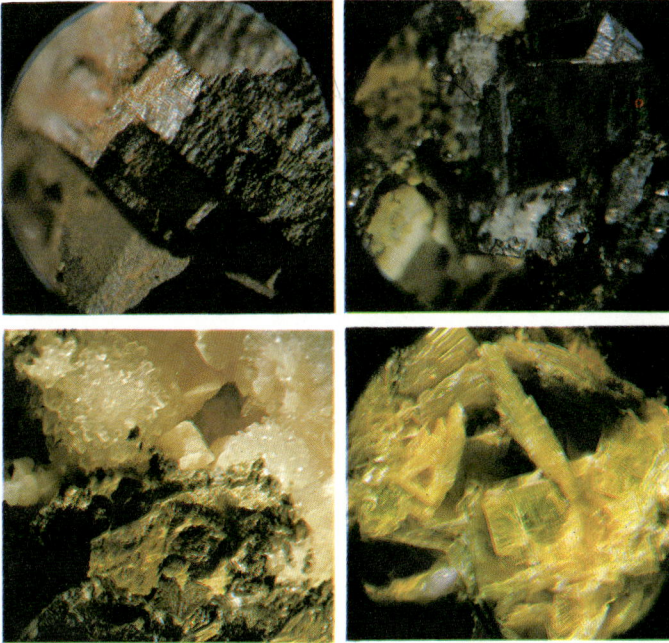

Metal mixtures

Above: Two (or more) metals may mix together to form alloys in a number of ways.
1. The metals may dissolve completely into one another. No trace of either pure metal can be seen under the microscope.
2. The metals may partly dissolve into one another. This often results in two types of crystal, each containing mainly one metal with traces of the other.
3. The two metals may be completely insoluble. Then crystals of one metal are embedded in the other.

It is perhaps odd that, with a few exceptions, pure metals are not so useful as impure ones. Most pure metals are soft and comparatively weak. Yet, when traces of another metal or non-metal are added to them, they generally become harder and stronger. We call this metal mixture an alloy.

Alloys

Iron, for example, can be greatly strengthened by the addition of less than two parts in 1000 (0.2 per cent) of carbon. Its hardness increases from about 100 to 130, and its tensile strength from about 20 to 30. It becomes the alloy known as mild steel.

Adding traces of copper to aluminium has an even more dramatic effect. When about 4 per cent of copper is added, the hardness of the aluminium leaps from less than 30 to over 100, and the tensile strength is quadrupled to become similar to that of mild steel! The alloy formed is known as duralumin. It is a particularly interesting alloy because it develops its strength and hardness slowly over a period of several days. This property is called age-hardening.

If they could not be alloyed, iron and aluminium would not be nearly so useful. The same goes for other common metals such as copper, zinc, tin, lead, nickel and chromium, and less common ones like magnesium, titanium, zirconium, molybdenum and tungsten. Copper is a very important alloying element, being present in brass,

Brass is copper alloyed with zinc. Its uses include bearings, nuts and numerous machine parts.

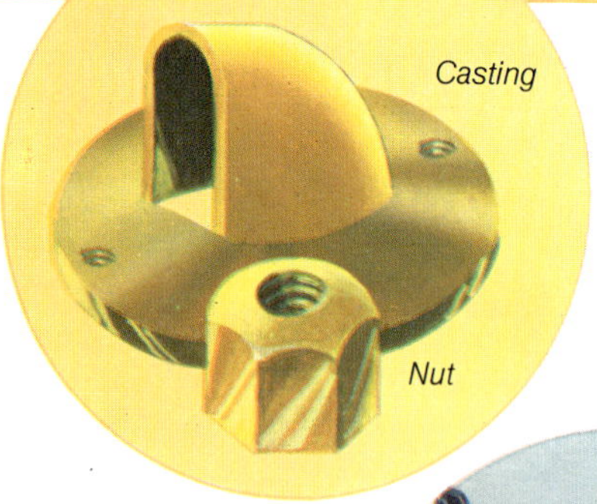

Bronze is copper alloyed with tin. It is used for all kinds of castings, including statues.

Cupronickel is copper alloyed with nickel. It is used in coins and turbine blades.

Duralumin is aluminium alloyed with copper and other metals. It is mainly used in aircraft construction.

German silver is copper alloyed with zinc and nickel. Its uses include ornaments and car trims.

bronze, gunmetal, cupronickel, German silver, and duralumin.

However, iron alloys – or steels – are the most important of all. By varying the amount of added carbon, a whole range of carbon steels are obtained, each with differing strengths, hardness and uses. Adding other metals as well as the traces of carbon to iron produces alloy steels. The metals may be added to improve the physical and/or the chemical properties. Alloy steel containing tungsten and chromium is exceptionally hard and keeps its hardness even when red hot. Alloy steel containing chromium and nickel does not rust – it is stainless steel.

Strength

It is perhaps easy to understand how adding one metal to another can change it chemically, but not so easy to understand why it should change physically. How is it that copper and zinc, which are both soft and weak, can be mixed to form brass, which is hard and strong? The answer lies in the crystal lattice *(see page 13)*, the basic unit from which the alloy is built up.

In copper the atoms are arranged in the lattice in a regular pattern. In brass, however, some of the larger zinc atoms have replaced some of the copper atoms. This distorts the lattice and makes it more difficult for layers of atoms to slip over one another. In other words it becomes stronger and harder. Carbon strengthens iron to form steel, but in a different way. Its atoms are small and can squeeze into the iron lattice. They strengthen it by preventing the layers of atoms from slipping easily.

Heat treatment

The properties of alloys, particularly steels, can be greatly modified by various heat treatments. One such treatment is called quenching. This involves plunging the red-hot metal into cold oil or water. It increases hardness but makes the metal brittle.

Tempering is a heat treatment that removes this brittleness without affecting the hardness. The quenched metal is reheated and allowed to cool very slowly.

Right: The spire of the Chrysler Building in New York, completed in 1930, is made of stainless steel and forms a very striking landmark.

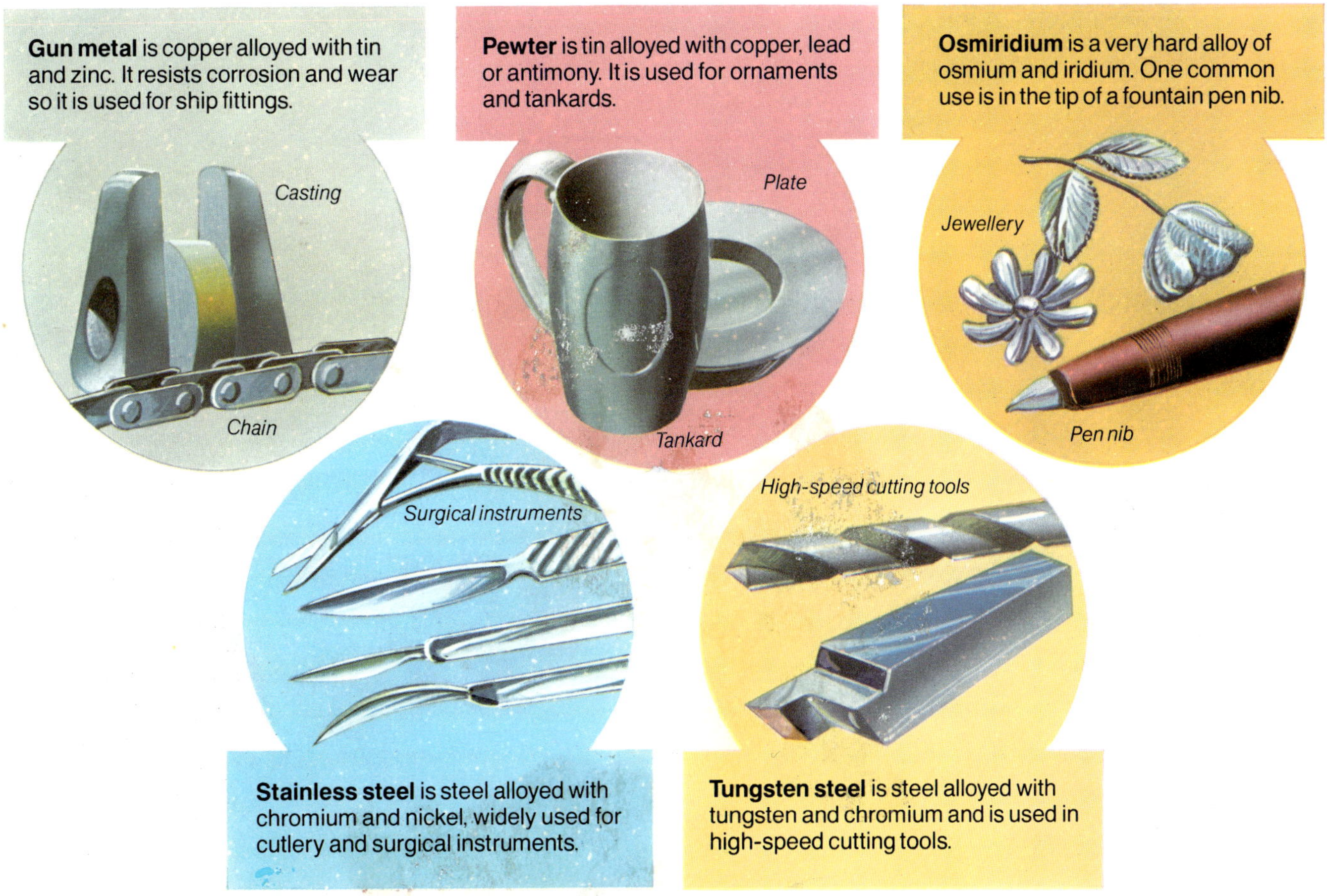

Gun metal is copper alloyed with tin and zinc. It resists corrosion and wear so it is used for ship fittings.

Casting
Chain

Pewter is tin alloyed with copper, lead or antimony. It is used for ornaments and tankards.

Plate
Tankard

Osmiridium is a very hard alloy of osmium and iridium. One common use is in the tip of a fountain pen nib.

Jewellery
Pen nib

Surgical instruments

Stainless steel is steel alloyed with chromium and nickel, widely used for cutlery and surgical instruments.

High-speed cutting tools

Tungsten steel is steel alloyed with tungsten and chromium and is used in high-speed cutting tools.

Metals under attack

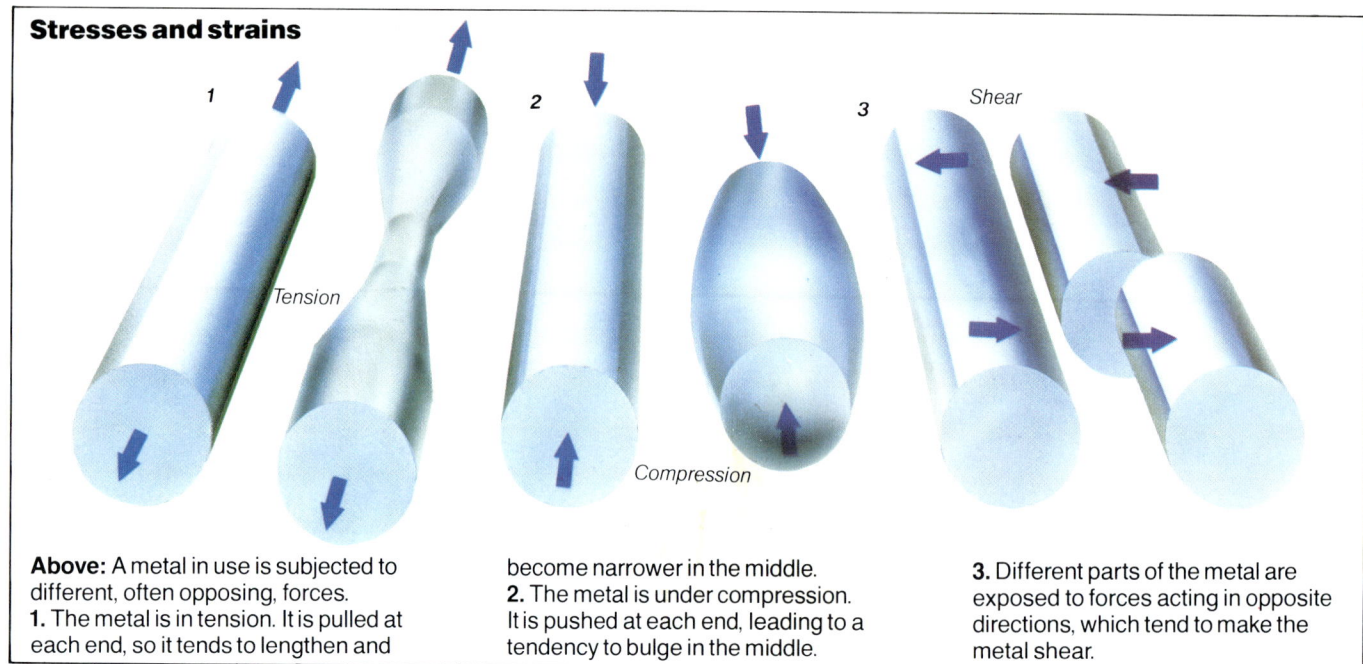

Stresses and strains

Above: A metal in use is subjected to different, often opposing, forces.
1. The metal is in tension. It is pulled at each end, so it tends to lengthen and become narrower in the middle.
2. The metal is under compression. It is pushed at each end, leading to a tendency to bulge in the middle.
3. Different parts of the metal are exposed to forces acting in opposite directions, which tend to make the metal shear.

From the moment that metals are put to work, they are exposed to attack from many quarters. For example, they are attacked by stresses, or forces, that try to stretch, compress or twist them out of shape. The connecting rod in a car engine experiences stretching (tension) when it is pulled down by the crankshaft. It experiences compression when the piston pushes it down. A car's prop shaft experiences twisting (shear) as it drives the wheels round.

Stress

Metals in general resist tensile, compressive, and shear stresses very well. They are also to some degree elastic, which allows them to 'give' slightly under a load but return to their original size when the load is removed. They are elastic, however, only up to a certain stress, called the elastic limit. Above this level metals do not return to their original size when the stress is removed and are therefore buckled. If the load is increased even more, there comes a point at which the metal will suddenly give and then break. This stress level is called the metal's ultimate strength.

For structural safety metals are chosen so that they will never normally be stressed beyond the elastic limit, which is way below their breaking strength. However, things are not quite so simple, for metals have been known to weaken and fail at unusually low stress levels. This has happened when the metal has been stressed repeatedly over a long period. The effect is known as metal fatigue, and it was first recognized as a serious problem when it caused the Comet aircraft disasters in 1954.

Corrosion

Metals also get attacked by their surroundings – by air, other gases, water and chemical solutions. If you leave bright iron nails outdoors for any length of time, they will quickly corrode. Air and moisture in the atmosphere combine to attack the iron at the surface, changing it to iron oxide, or rust. In a similar way the atmosphere attacks copper, converting it to blue-green copper carbonate. Aluminium, zinc, chromium and lead are among metals that are good at resisting corrosion.

Corrosion of exposed metal structures is worse in industrial areas where the sulphur dioxide in the atmosphere forms an acid which eats away the metal.

Right: This iron cannon, dating from the 1700s, shows the ravages of more than two centuries of salt-water corrosion.

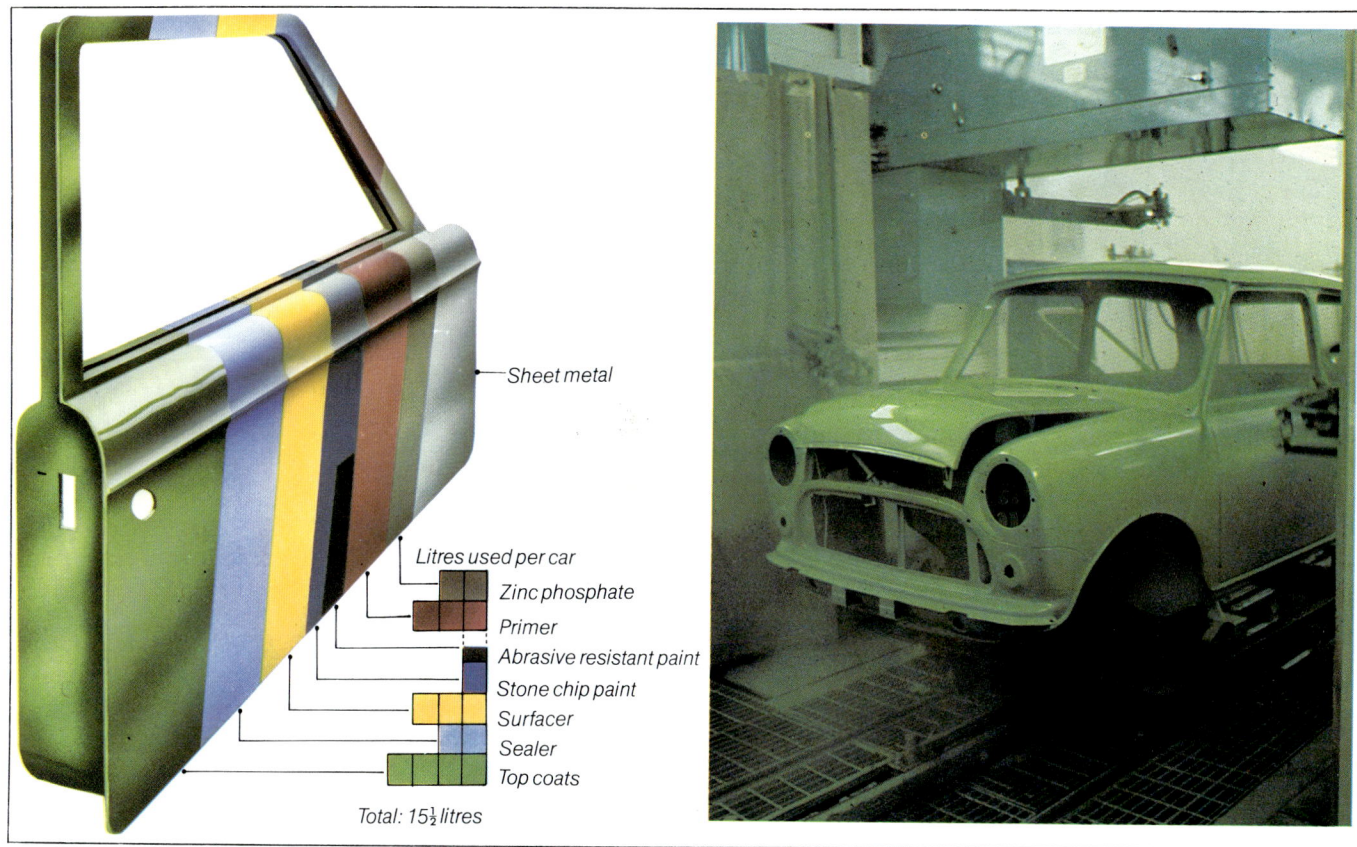

Above: To provide an in-depth protection against corrosion, mild steel car bodies receive several coatings of paint. The first is usually a phosphate corrosion-proofing coating applied by dipping the body shell in a paint vat. The other coats are applied by spraying.

Above right: A British Leyland Mini being sprayed in the automatic paint workshop.

Salt and water are a dangerous combination for metals. Salt solution is a much better conductor of electricity than salt alone. When it is in contact with iron it forms tiny electrical cells on the metallic surface. The iron becomes oxidized, forms rust, and eventually dissolves away. Corrosion here is an electrochemical reaction.

This is why cars and other metal objects rust badly when exposed to salty spray from the sea or in winter, when salt is spread on roads to prevent ice forming.

Protective measures

A metal may be protected against corrosion in a number of ways. For example, it can be painted. Paint forms a thin plastic film which prevents air and moisture from attacking the bare unprotected metal.

The metal can be coated with another metal that does not corrode. Steel, for example, can be coated with zinc, a process known as galvanizing. It can also be coated with chromium ('chromium plate') or tin ('tinplate') for protection. This is done by electroplating. The coating is deposited on the base metal by electrolysis, the object being dipped into an electrolytic solution of chromium or tin.

Another approach to the problem is to alloy the corrodable metal with other metals that resist corrosion. This is how non-rusting, stainless steel is made.

Left: Prolonged exposure to very low temperatures, as here in Antarctica, can make metals brittle and weak.

Testing and measuring metal

The modern engineer has the choice of a great variety of metals and alloys when designing machines and structures. He calculates the forces, or stresses, each part of the design will have to withstand in practice. Then he selects for each component a metal with suitable properties – strength, hardness, ductility, resistance to corrosion, etc.

He may use existing metals whose strength or hardness is known. Their properties are known from tests carried out on specimens of similar composition. If no suitable metal is available, the design engineer may have metals specially made to give the combination of properties he desires. He then tests specimens of the new metal to check that it performs as well as it should.

Destructive testing
To find their basic mechanical properties, samples of metals are tested to destruction on a variety of apparatus. One of the commonest tests is the tensile test. A bar of the sample metal is stretched in a machine which can apply variable loads to it. For each load, the amount of stretch is recorded. Ever increasing loads are applied until the bar breaks.

When the load applied (termed stress) is plotted on a graph against the stretch produced (strain), a characteristic curve is obtained. This describes the behaviour of the metal under load, and shows the pull needed to permanently stretch and finally break the bar. The stress needed to break the bar is known as the ultimate, or tensile, strength of the metal. The tensile strength of mild steel is about 5 tonnes per square centimetre, whereas that of pure aluminium is only 20 per cent of this.

Test samples are also tested for hardness. A machine presses a steel ball or a diamond pyramid into the surface of the metal for a given time, and the area dented is measured. The harder the metal is, the smaller the area of indentation. Hardness is measured as a number on the Brinell scale. This gives a hardness of 130 for mild steel but less than 30 for pure aluminium.

Another standard test determines the breaking strength of a metal under sharp impact. Metals behave differently under sudden impact than they do under a gradual load. In the common Izod test, a notched metal bar is struck by a heavy pendulum until it fractures.

Non-destructive testing
These methods of destructive testing cannot, of course, be carried out on metal parts which the designer actually uses. And if these need to be checked, non-destructive methods must be used. They include examination by X-rays or ultrasonic (sonar) techniques which produce shadow pictures that can show up defects in the metal. Otherwise invisible cracks and flaws on the metal surface can be shown up by applying penetrating, often fluorescent, dye. When the excess dye is removed, the dye retained in the cracks can be easily detected.

Testing is carried out not only on test specimens and individual parts, but also on machines and structures as a

Concorde fatigue test unit

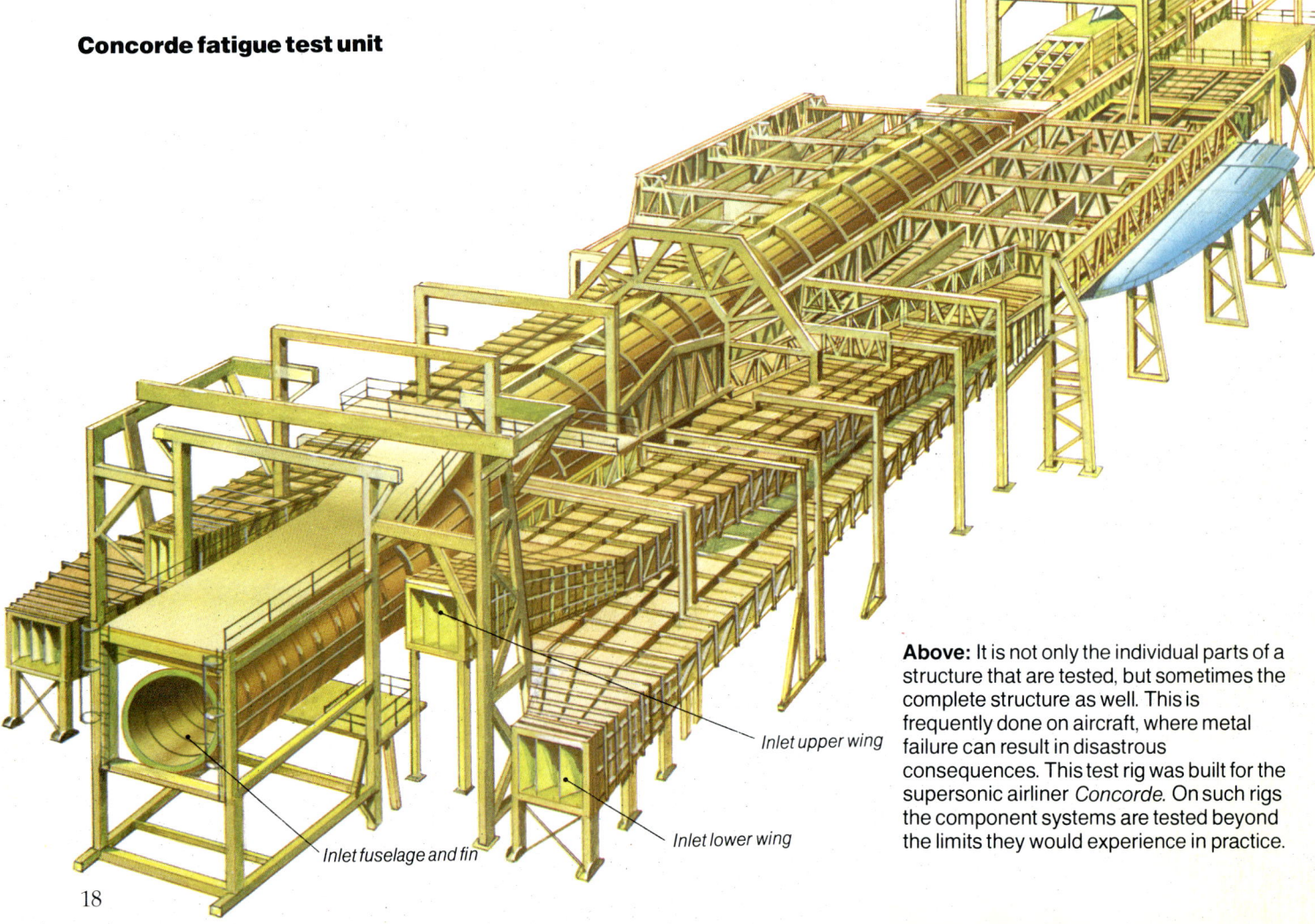

Inlet fuselage and fin
Inlet lower wing
Inlet upper wing

Above: It is not only the individual parts of a structure that are tested, but sometimes the complete structure as well. This is frequently done on aircraft, where metal failure can result in disastrous consequences. This test rig was built for the supersonic airliner *Concorde*. On such rigs the component systems are tested beyond the limits they would experience in practice.

Right: Ultrasonic testing equipment is being used here to examine nuclear reactor fuel pins.

whole. A good example of this is the fatigue testing of airframes (aeroplane bodies). Whole airframes are tested in specially-built laboratories under conditions similar to those experienced in flight. Hydraulic jacks impose varying loads at different points. Infra-red heaters provide surface heating, and liquid nitrogen surface cooling. In thousands of hours of testing, the airframe is made to experience the rapidly changing loads and temperatures the real aircraft undergoes when it takes off, cruises at high altitude and lands. These tests are conducted both with a simulated full load of passengers and cargo, and also when empty.

Below: The micrometer, feeler gauges and calipers are all instruments commonly used for measuring dimensions of metal objects.

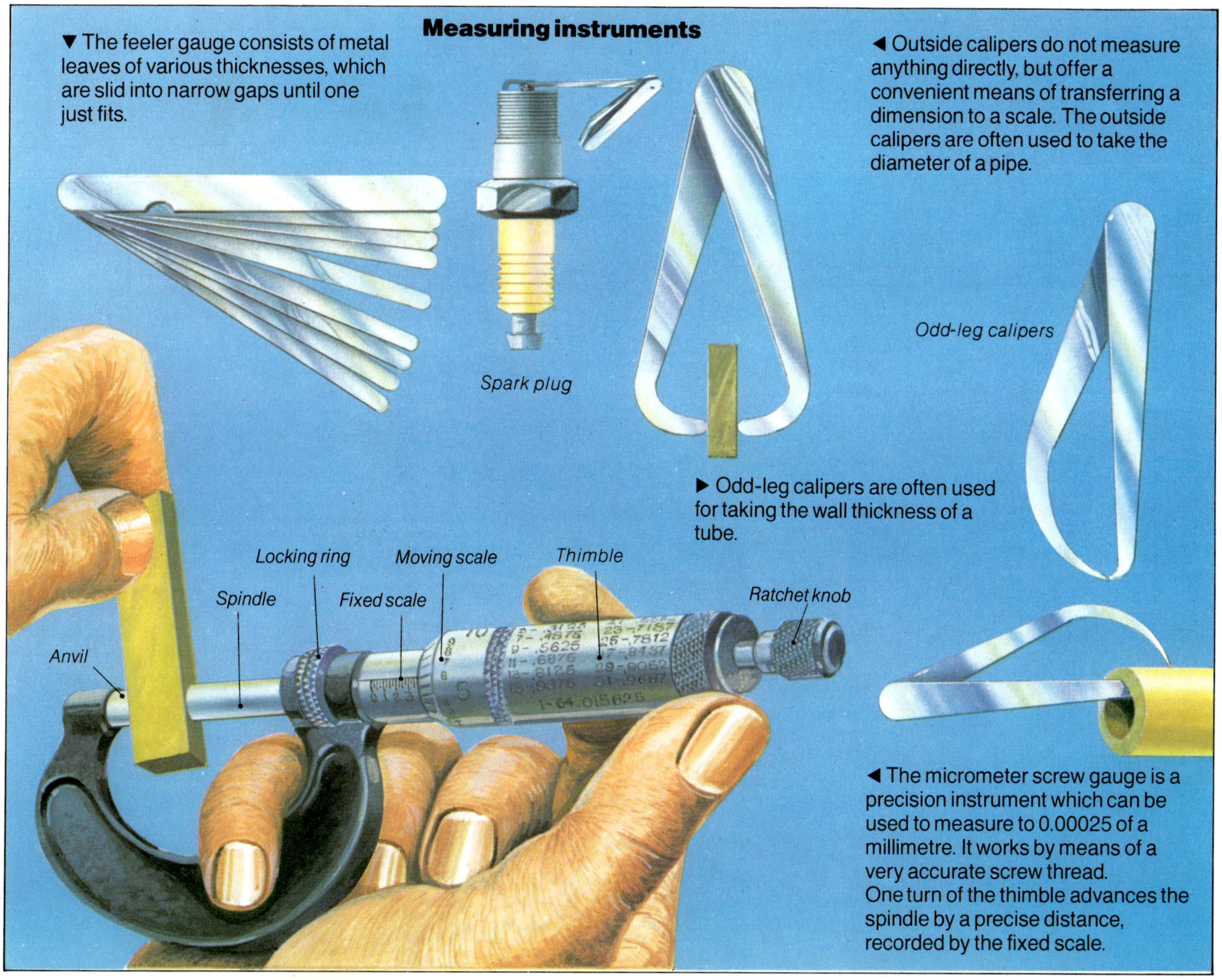

Measuring instruments

▼ The feeler gauge consists of metal leaves of various thicknesses, which are slid into narrow gaps until one just fits.

Spark plug

◀ Outside calipers do not measure anything directly, but offer a convenient means of transferring a dimension to a scale. The outside calipers are often used to take the diameter of a pipe.

Odd-leg calipers

▶ Odd-leg calipers are often used for taking the wall thickness of a tube.

Anvil — Spindle — Locking ring — Fixed scale — Moving scale — Thimble — Ratchet knob

◀ The micrometer screw gauge is a precision instrument which can be used to measure to 0.00025 of a millimetre. It works by means of a very accurate screw thread. One turn of the thimble advances the spindle by a precise distance, recorded by the fixed scale.

Sources of metals

Most metals do not occur in the form of metal in the Earth's crust because they combine too readily with other chemical elements. They are found in this combined state in a variety of minerals. Aluminium, iron, magnesium and titanium, for example, are found most commonly as oxides (combined with oxygen).

Metallic minerals are in general scattered sparsely among the rocks that make up the Earth's crust. Only in certain locations have natural geological processes concentrated them. When the concentrated deposits can be profitably mined and processed to extract the metals they contain, they are known as ores.

Native metals

A few metals do occur naturally, or native, in the Earth's crust, including copper, gold, silver and platinum. Gold, silver and platinum do not combine readily with other elements and tend to remain in the metallic state in the rocks. Copper is more reactive, but it can be found native if conditions are right. These metals again occur sparsely in the rocks and only when natural geological processes have concentrated them can they be profitably worked.

Generally the native metals are found as relatively small grains and only occasionally do large nuggets occur. In the Lake Superior region of North America copper nuggets weighing several tonnes have been discovered. Australian gold mines have yielded a number of nuggets weighing over 45 kilograms, including the remarkably pure 'Welcome Stranger', discovered in 1869, which weighed 70 kilograms.

Origin of ores

There are several ways in which minerals can become concentrated into exploitable ore deposits. Concentration may take place during the actual rock formation process while the magma (molten rock) is cooling. The large magnetite (iron ore) deposits in Kiruna, northern Sweden, were formed in this way.

As magma progressively solidifies, the mineral-rich fluid remaining becomes more mobile. It can penetrate and dissolve away existing rocks and replace them with new minerals. Finally the fluid becomes a hot-water solution charged with gas. This hydrothermal solution forces its way into cracks in the rocks where it cools and deposits the minerals it contains as rich veins. Zinc, lead and copper ores are frequently found in similar veins.

When rocks become exposed in surface outcrops by land movements, they are gradually worn away by the action of the weather or flowing water. The minerals they contain may then be transported and deposited elsewhere. During this process heavy minerals and native metals are often concentrated into what are known as placer deposits. Gold and platinum are worked from placer deposits, as is cassiterite, the heavy ore of tin.

Some minerals are dissolved during weathering and accumulate as solutions in seawater. Ore deposits form when they are precipitated from this solution. Many copper, iron and manganese ore deposits were formed in this way, including the huge Chiaturi deposit of manganese in the Caucasus region of the USSR.

World production of metals

Iron (million tonnes)
Aluminium (million tonnes)
Manganese (thousand tonnes)
Platinum (million troy ounces)
Chrome (thousand tonnes)
Copper (thousand tonnes)
Zinc (thousand tonnes)
Lead (thousand tonnes)
Gold (thousand kilograms)
Nickel (thousand tonnes)
Silver (million troy ounces)
Mercury (thousand flasks)
Tin (thousand tonnes)
Molybdenum (thousand tonnes)
Tungsten (thousand tonnes)
Cobalt (thousand tonnes)
Uranium (thousand tonnes)

Canada 10.3, 1,247, 647
U.S.A. 79, 1,351, 1.8
Mexico 5.1, 475
Central America 2.8, 2.4
West Indies 18
Guyana 3.5
Colombia 8, 0.25
Peru 354, 458, 179
Bolivia 31, 60, 18
Brazil 9.6, 800
Chile 1,035
Argentina 37, 30, 11.8

Metals in the Earth's crust

Above: Metals occur worldwide, and some countries have very large deposits. Production figures (1980) for 17 major metals have been broken down to show the distribution amongst the major mining areas.

Right: Six metals (aluminium, iron, calcium, sodium, potassium, and magnesium) make up just 24 per cent of the Earth's crust. Oxygen and silicon comprise over 74 per cent, leaving the other 84 elements accounting for less than 2 per cent.

Mining methods

After farming, mining is the world's oldest industry and vies with farming as being the most important. Man began deliberately mining minerals in about 3500 BC, when he discovered how to smelt bronze. At first he used the ore deposits he found on the surface, then later followed them underground. Ores are still mined by both surface and underground methods today.

The quantities of ores now mined are staggeringly high. The United States

Left: In particularly hard strata, the ore-bearing rock has to be blasted loose. Here, gold miners are preparing a rock face for blasting. The face has been drilled and explosive is being packed into the holes prior to detonation.

Left: In the 'gold rush' days in North America and Australia in the late 19th century, prospectors would 'pan' streams for gold. The lighter gravelly material would be washed away, while any gold present, being heavy, would tend to remain behind.

Right: Most tin ore (cassiterite) is extracted from lake and offshore deposits, as here near Kuala Lumpur in Malaysia. Massive floating dredges are used to scoop up the ore and gravel mixture.

and Russia between them extract about 300 million tonnes of iron ore each year, while world production is practically double this figure. Such vast amounts of different ores are being mined that there could soon be a grave shortage of metals (*see page 42*).

Surface mining

Mining on the surface, often called opencast mining, is considerably cheaper than mining underground. Fortunately many major ore bodies do occur at or near the surface. Most bauxite (aluminium ore) and iron and copper ores are mined at the surface. Some opencast mines cover vast areas. The Bingham Canyon copper mine in Utah, USA, covers over 7 square kilometres and has been excavated to a depth of nearly 800 metres.

Mining begins by stripping off any earth and rock, called overburden, that lies on top of the deposit. Some of the world's largest excavators are used for this purpose. If the exposed deposit is relatively soft, it can be removed by power shovels or rotary excavators and loaded into trucks or railway wagons. If the deposit is hard, it must first be broken up by blasting with explosives.

Different techniques are required to extract the minerals found in placer deposits such as cassiterite (tin ore) and gold. Vast deposits of cassiterite mixed with gravel occur in Malaysia and Indonesia, both onshore and offshore. They are mined by huge dredgers, which can extract and sort thousands of tonnes of gravel a day.

Dredging may also be used where gold placers occur. Or the gold-bearing gravel may be washed through sluice-boxes containing bars, or riffles, which tend to trap any heavy gold particles passing through. Lighter particles are carried away by the water. Where the placer gravels are dry, miners use powerful water jets to break up the gravel and wash it through sluice-boxes. This is termed hydraulic mining.

Mining underground

When an ore body occurs deep underground, a vertical shaft is sunk to it. Miners blast horizontal tunnels out from the shaft as they work.

In a mature mine the tunnels can extend for hundreds and even thousands of kilometres at different levels. And if an ore vein is rich, it may be followed down to great depths. Currently in South Africa gold mines are being worked at depths of over 3,800 metres, where rock temperatures can reach over 50°C.

In most mines the miners usually have to blast the ore free from the rock with explosives. They drill a pattern of holes in the rock face with pneumatic drills, either hand-held or mounted on a carriage. They insert 'shots' of explosive (usually ammonium nitrate mixed with fuel oil), and detonate them. They then load the broken ore into railway wagons for removal. In many modern mines, if space permits, mechanical loaders are used.

The mining technique used depends on the precise location and nature of the ore body. If the ore deposit is firm, thick and level, 'rooms' can be excavated in it, leaving pillars here and there to support the roof. In other situations, however, extensive shoring of the excavated tunnels may be necessary to prevent rock fall. But, wherever it is, underground mining is a dangerous business.

Below: This vast man-made pit, nearly 800 metres deep, is the Bingham Canyon copper mine in Utah, USA. More than 8 million tonnes of ore have been extracted since mining began here.

From mine to metal

Steelmaking

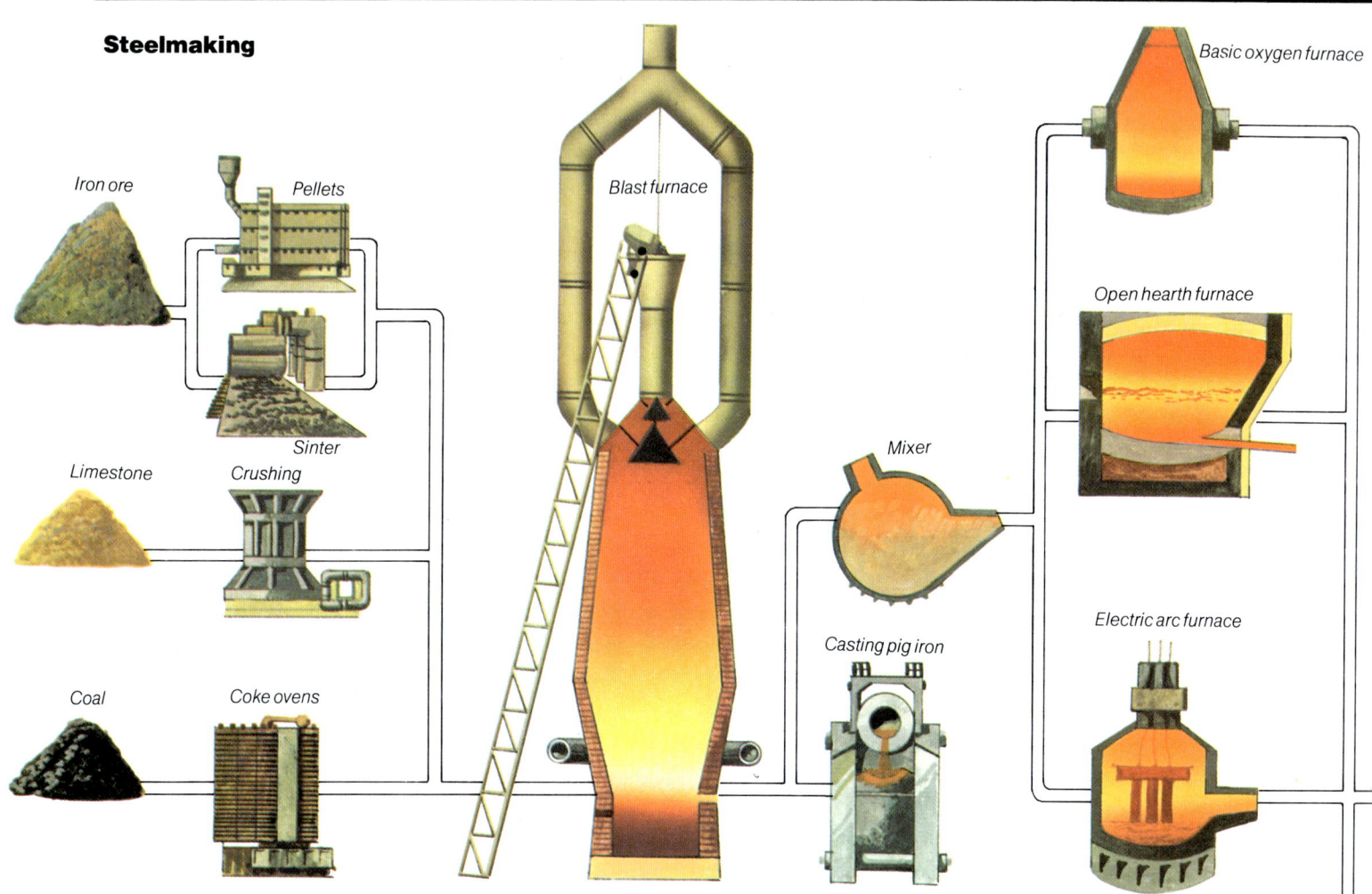

Mineral dressing

Most mined ores are mixed up with a certain amount of earth or rock – unwanted material known as gangue. If there is more than a little gangue present, as much as possible has to be removed before the ore goes for processing into metal. The process of concentrating an ore is known as benefication, and the means of doing so, mineral dressing. The methods of mineral dressing chosen depend on the ore being treated.

Usually the ore is first crushed into small lumps and sometimes powder. If the wanted mineral is much heavier than the gangue, it can be separated by gravity methods, such as washing with flowing water, which carries the lighter particles away. If the ore mineral is magnetic, it can be removed by a magnet.

Advantage can also be taken of a mineral's wetting properties in a frothing liquid – a method known as flotation. The finely-divided ore particles attach themselves to the bubbles in the froth, which is then skimmed off. When the ore contains a mixture of minerals, successive flotation treatments may be required to separate them. For example, in the treatment of the copper-nickel sulphide ore from the rich mines at Sudbury, Canada, flotation is first used to separate the copper and nickel sulphides from other gangue minerals, and then used to separate the copper sulphide from the nickel sulphide.

Flotation and other mineral dressing operations often break down the ore into very fine particles. Left like this it would be difficult to handle and would soon clog up the machinery used in subsequent processes. It is therefore sintered, or heated strongly in a grate, after being mixed with a fuel such as coke. This treatment converts it into porous lumps called sinter, which are easier to handle.

Extracting the metal

Methods of extracting metals from their concentrated ores varies from metal to metal. Extraction by means of heat, or smelting, is by far the most widely used method. Iron, copper, lead, zinc and tin are common metals obtained by smelting in high-temperature furnaces. Ores may also be converted into metal by electrical and chemical methods (see page 28). Aluminium is extracted by electricity from a molten solution of its ore. Many copper ores are extracted by chemical means.

Smelting and the other extraction methods invariably convert the ore into a metal that contains far too many impurities to be useful. So this crude metal has to be refined, or purified. This can be done in various ways, by further furnace treatment, by electrical or chemical methods, or by a combination of both. In many cases the impurities are worthless and are discarded. But sometimes the impurities may be very valuable indeed. In the case of the Sudbury ore mentioned earlier, the 'impurities' include silver, gold and the even more precious platinum group metals.

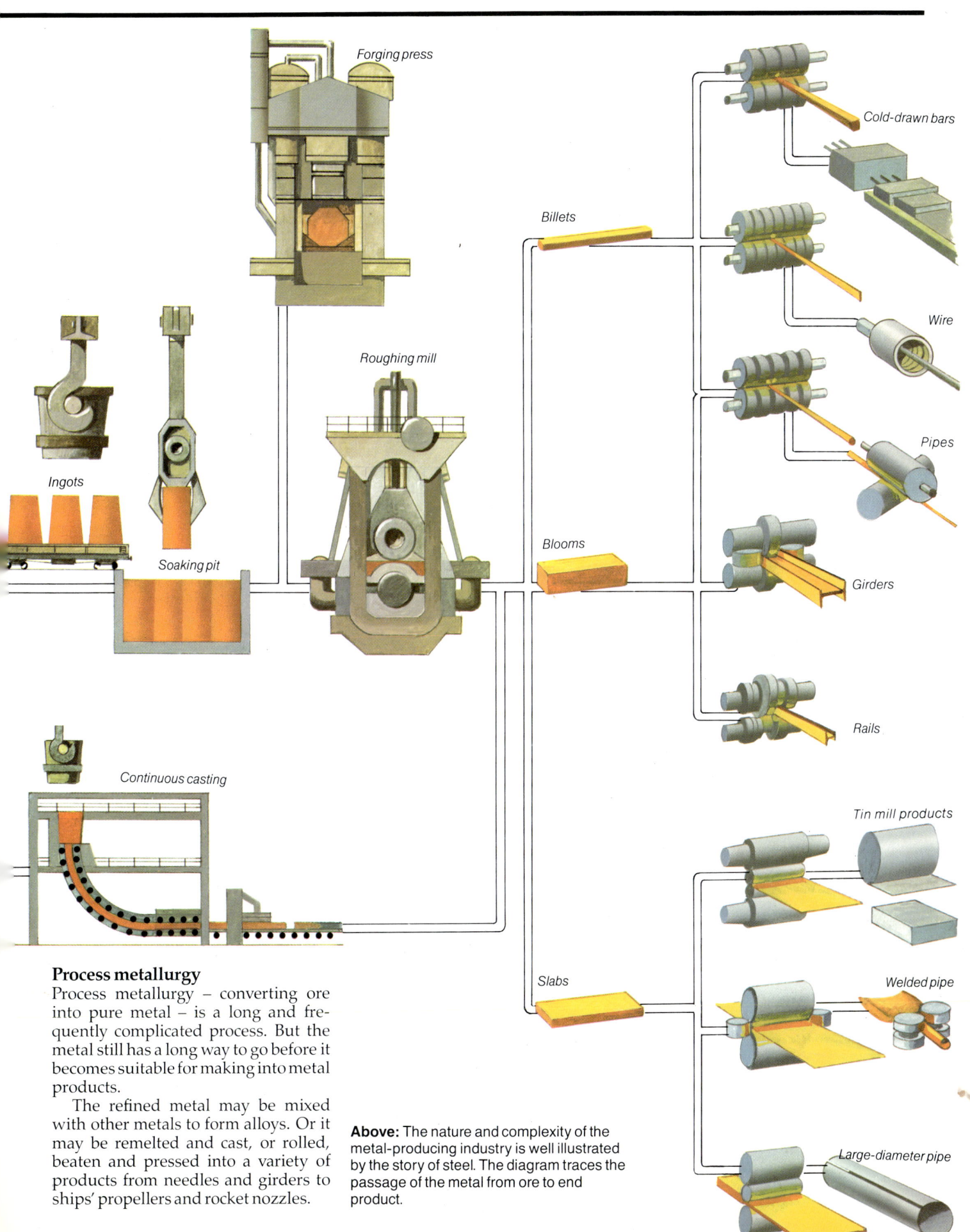

Process metallurgy

Process metallurgy – converting ore into pure metal – is a long and frequently complicated process. But the metal still has a long way to go before it becomes suitable for making into metal products.

The refined metal may be mixed with other metals to form alloys. Or it may be remelted and cast, or rolled, beaten and pressed into a variety of products from needles and girders to ships' propellers and rocket nozzles.

Above: The nature and complexity of the metal-producing industry is well illustrated by the story of steel. The diagram traces the passage of the metal from ore to end product.

Smelting the ore

Above: The tapping of a blast furnace looks spectacular as the white-hot molten metal pours out.

Blast furnace

Above: In the blast furnace iron ore, coke and limestone are loaded into a refractory-lined tower and heated to a temperature of about 1600°C in a hot-air blast. The iron ore melts and the impurities react with the limestone to form a slag which collects on top of the denser molten iron.

The original and still most widely used method of obtaining metals from their ores is smelting – heating them fiercely in a furnace. Another name for this kind of operation is pyro-metallurgy; 'pyro' means 'fire'. The best-known example of smelting is provided by the blast-furnace smelting of iron ores. The furnace is so-called because air is blasted through it.

The iron blast-furnace is a tall steel tower, lined with refractory (heat-resistant) bricks on the inside. The latest furnaces are huge – over 60 metres high, with a base, or hearth, over 10 metres in diameter. They operate continuously and can produce 8,000 tonnes or more every 24 hours. Blast furnaces are also used to smelt lead, zinc and tin from their ores, but these are much smaller.

Smelting iron

The main ores smelted in the blast furnace are iron oxides, such as haematite and magnetite. They are usually first concentrated in mineral dressing operations. Some ores are rich enough to smelt directly.

In the furnace the ore is heated strongly with coke and limestone. Coke plays three roles in the process. First, it is fuel to heat up the furnace to 1600°C or more. Secondly, it reacts chemically with the iron ore. Thirdly, it supports the material in the furnace. The limestone is added to absorb impurities in the ore.

The raw materials are loaded into the top of the furnace through a 'double-bell' valve system, which acts as a gas trap. Hot air is blasted through nozzles (tuyères) near the base of the furnace and makes the coke burn fiercely. The hot coke, which is mainly carbon, combines with the oxygen in the ore, reducing it to iron. Because of the temperature inside the furnace (1600°C), the iron melts and trickles down to the hearth (base).

26

Right: An industrial area in France showing a group of blast furnaces. Alongside them are hot-blast stoves, which are brickwork chambers that preheat the air before it is blasted into the furnaces.

Meanwhile, impurities present in the iron ore combine with the limestone to form a liquid slag, which also trickles down to the hearth and forms a layer on top of the denser iron. Carbon monoxide and other gases are drawn off from the top of the furnace.

These gases are too precious to be wasted, so they are used to heat the air blast for the furnace. The gases are first cleaned by being passed through dust catchers and spray chambers. In the next stage they are burned in hot-blast stoves which are lined with refractory brickwork that absorbs the heat. Air is then forced through the stoves and is thus heated. Several hot-blast stoves serve each blast furnace. Whilst one is preheating the air, others will be being heated by the hot gases.

The blast furnace operates continuously day and night until its lining wears out, which does not happen for several years. Periodically the furnace is tapped, or opened, to withdraw the molten iron and slag. In the past the molten iron was run into a trough and thence into small moulds alongside. This was once likened to a sow feeding its piglets, and the iron produced became known as pig iron. Some pig iron is still first cast into moulds, but most of it is conveyed by huge travelling ladles direct to refining furnaces to be made into steel.

Other ores

The most common lead and zinc ores, galena and zinc blende, are not oxides, but sulphides. Before they can be smelted in the blast furnace they have to be roasted in air. Roasting changes the sulphides to oxides, which the blast furnace can handle. Since zinc has a low boiling point, it is removed as a vapour from the top of the blast furnace. It is condensed in a shower of molten lead, and later separates as a layer on top of the lead.

Right: The extraction of nickel from its ores, which usually contain copper and iron as well, is a complicated process. It involves many stages of concentration and purification.

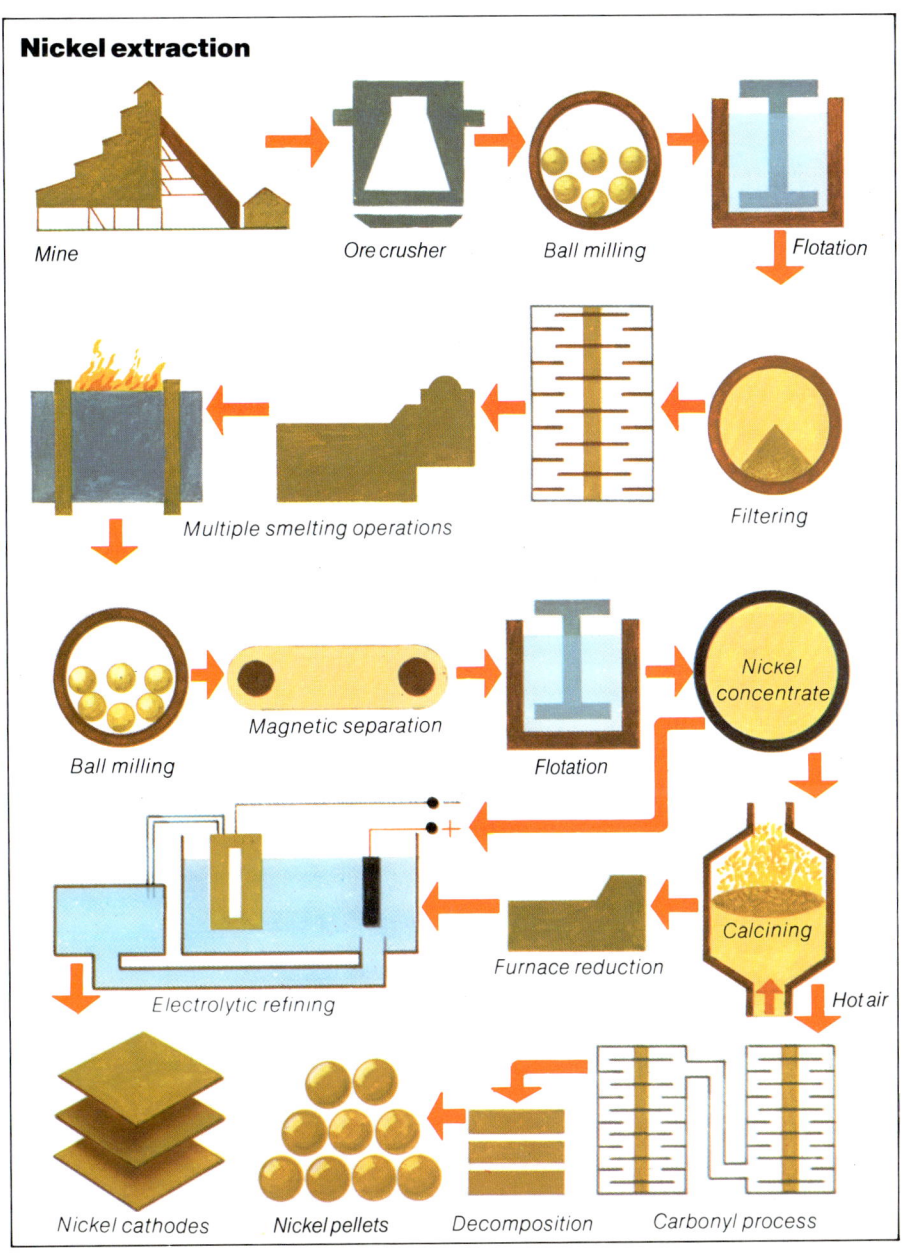

Nickel extraction

27

Electrochemical extraction

Downs cell

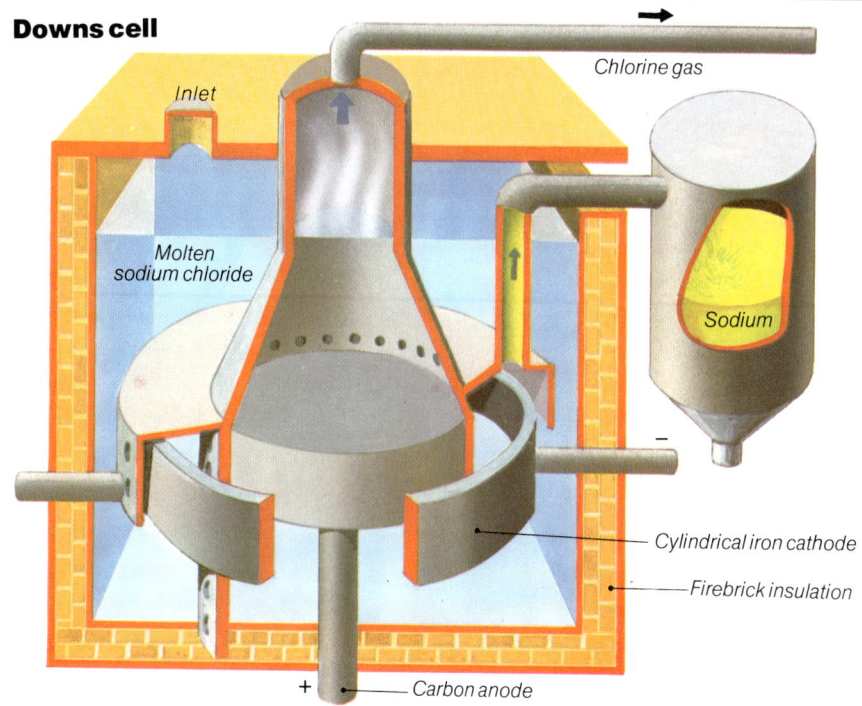

Left: In the Downs cell, sodium is prepared by the electrolysis of molten sodium chloride. Sodium was the first metal prepared by electrolysis, by Sir Humphry Davy in 1807.

Unlike most other common metals, aluminium is not extracted from its ore by smelting. It is produced instead by means of electrolysis. Magnesium, sodium and potassium are also produced in this way. The English chemist Humphry Davy pioneered the electrolytic method of metal production by preparing potassium and sodium for the first time in the early 1800s. Electrolysis is a way of using electricity to split a chemical compound into its constituent elements. The compound can be electrolysed either when it is in solution or in the molten state.

Sodium

Sodium metal is produced by the electrolysis of molten sodium chloride. Sodium chloride, better known as common salt, is a kind of chemical compound called a salt. One feature of a salt is that in solution and when it is molten, it splits up into ions. Ions are atoms which have lost or gained electrons to become electrically charged. Sodium chloride splits into positively-charged sodium ions (Na^+) and negatively-charged chlorine ions (Cl^-). Sodium and all metal ions are always positively charged.

Electricity is passed through electrodes into the bath, or cell, containing the molten sodium chloride. The positive electrode is called the anode, and the negative one the cathode. In electricity positive charges attract negative charges and vice versa. So in the cell the anode attracts the negative chlorine ions, while the cathode attracts the positive sodium ions. This results in chlorine gas being set free at the anode and molten sodium metal forming at the cathode. The gas is then siphoned off.

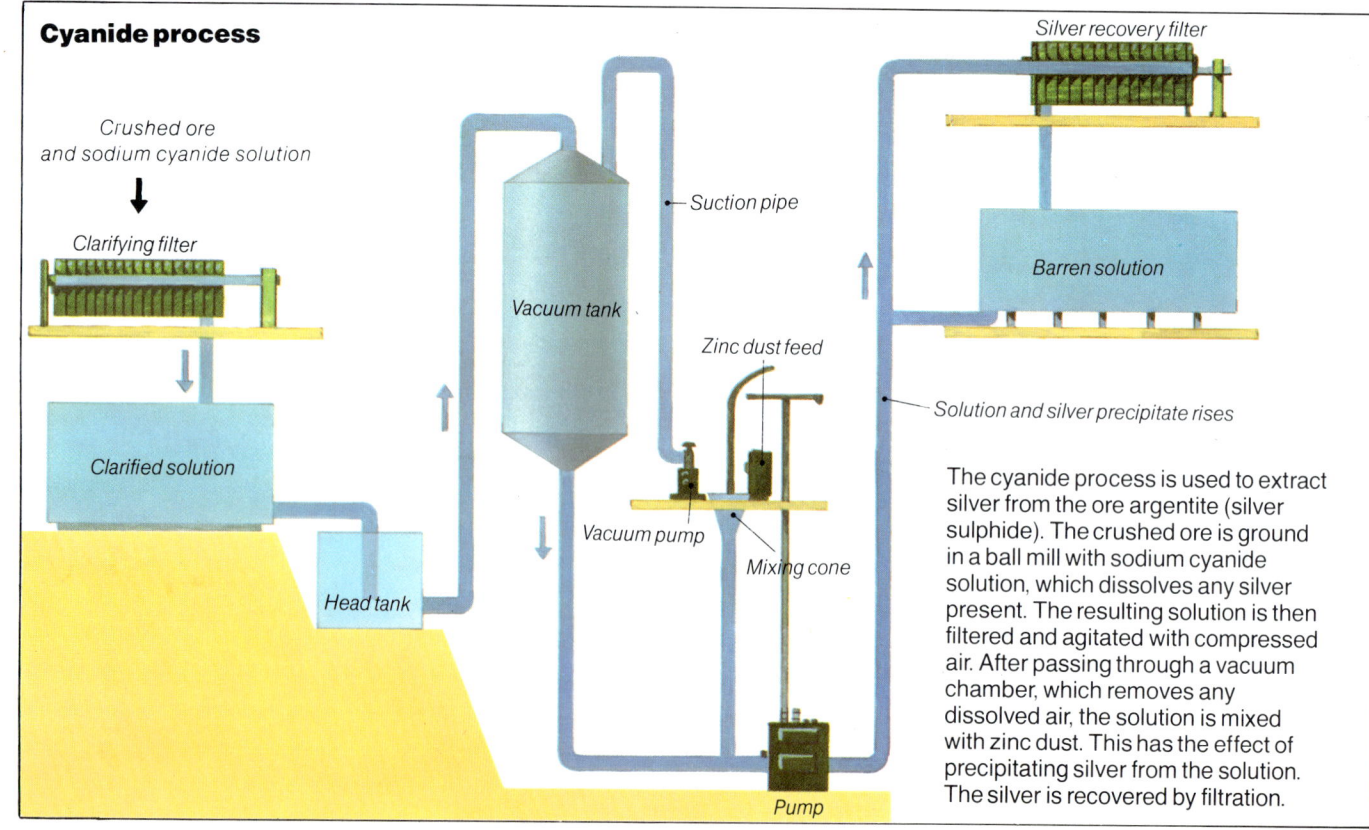

The cyanide process is used to extract silver from the ore argentite (silver sulphide). The crushed ore is ground in a ball mill with sodium cyanide solution, which dissolves any silver present. The resulting solution is then filtered and agitated with compressed air. After passing through a vacuum chamber, which removes any dissolved air, the solution is mixed with zinc dust. This has the effect of precipitating silver from the solution. The silver is recovered by filtration.

Right: Electrolysis plays a major role in the extraction of copper from its ore. It is used to purify copper obtained by smelting, as here, or for extracting copper from a solution after leaching the ore.

Aluminium

In the case of aluminium the purified ore is electrolysed in a molten solution. The method is known as the Hall-Héroult process after its co-inventors. In the process pure alumina (aluminium oxide) is dissolved in molten cryolite (another aluminium mineral). This is done to reduce the temperature to a reasonable level (about 950°C). Alumina itself does not melt until over 2000°C! The molten minerals are contained in a cell, lined with graphite (carbon), which acts as the cathode. Carbon rods dip into the molten liquid to form the anodes. Molten aluminium collects on the cathode floor of the cell, while oxygen is produced at the anodes.

Leaching

Some minerals are better extracted from their ores by treatment with chemical solutions, a process known as leaching. Copper oxide ores such as cuprite are often treated in this way. They are washed with a sulphuric acid solution. The acid dissolves the copper oxide, forming copper sulphate, leaving the associated gangue behind.

The copper sulphate solution is then purified to rid it of, for example, iron sulphate. Copper metal is then obtained from the purified solution by electrolysis.

Leaching is also a major method of extracting uranium, gold, and silver from their ores. Sulphuric acid is often used to leach uranium. Gold and silver are extracted by leaching with sodium cyanide.

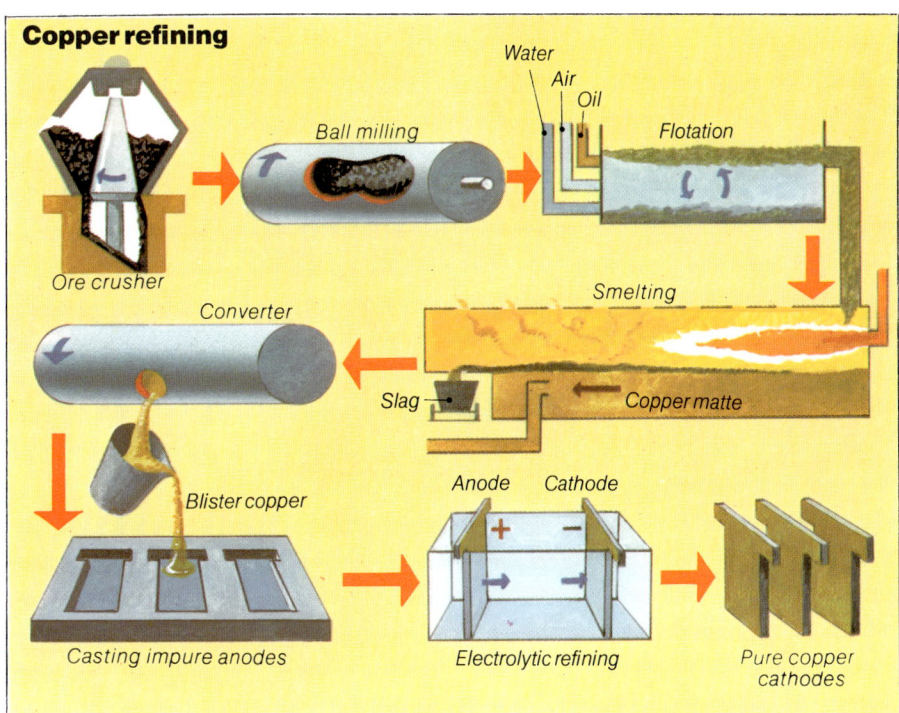

Copper refining

Below: This large magnesium extraction plant is in Japan. The huge settling tanks can be seen in the foreground.

29

Refining methods

Left: An electric arc furnace is here being loaded with steel scrap.

Right: Molten metal is progressively cooled as it passes through a chamber lined with high-velocity jets of water.

We have seen how metals are extracted from their ores by the use of heat (in smelting), electricity (in electrolysis) or chemicals (in leaching). Heat, electricity or chemicals can also be used to purify, or refine, the resulting impure metals.

Steelmaking

Steel is produced by purifying blast-furnace pig iron with heat in different kinds of furnaces. Pig iron is too impure to be useful in itself. The carbon content makes iron very brittle. Thus refining processes concentrate on removing most of the carbon. But not all of it is removed, because pure iron is too soft and weak. Iron containing traces of carbon (0·2 – 1·5 per cent) is hard and strong. This is the alloy known as steel.

Three main processes are used to refine pig iron – basic-oxygen, electric-arc and open-hearth (in order of importance). The basic-oxygen furnace, or converter, is a large conical vessel. Molten pig iron is poured into it, together with steel scrap and lime. A jet of pure oxygen is then directed at supersonic speed onto the molten metal from a tube, or lance. The oxygen jet penetrates the metal and burns out the carbon. Other impurities in the metal combine with the lime to form a slag. In about 40 minutes the process is finished, and the molten steel and slag are poured off separately by tilting the converter.

In the open-hearth process molten steel, scrap and lime are loaded into a shallow hearth furnace, heated by burning gas or oil in a constant supply of hot air. Once the predominant method of steelmaking, the open-hearth process has been superseded because it takes about 10 hours to make

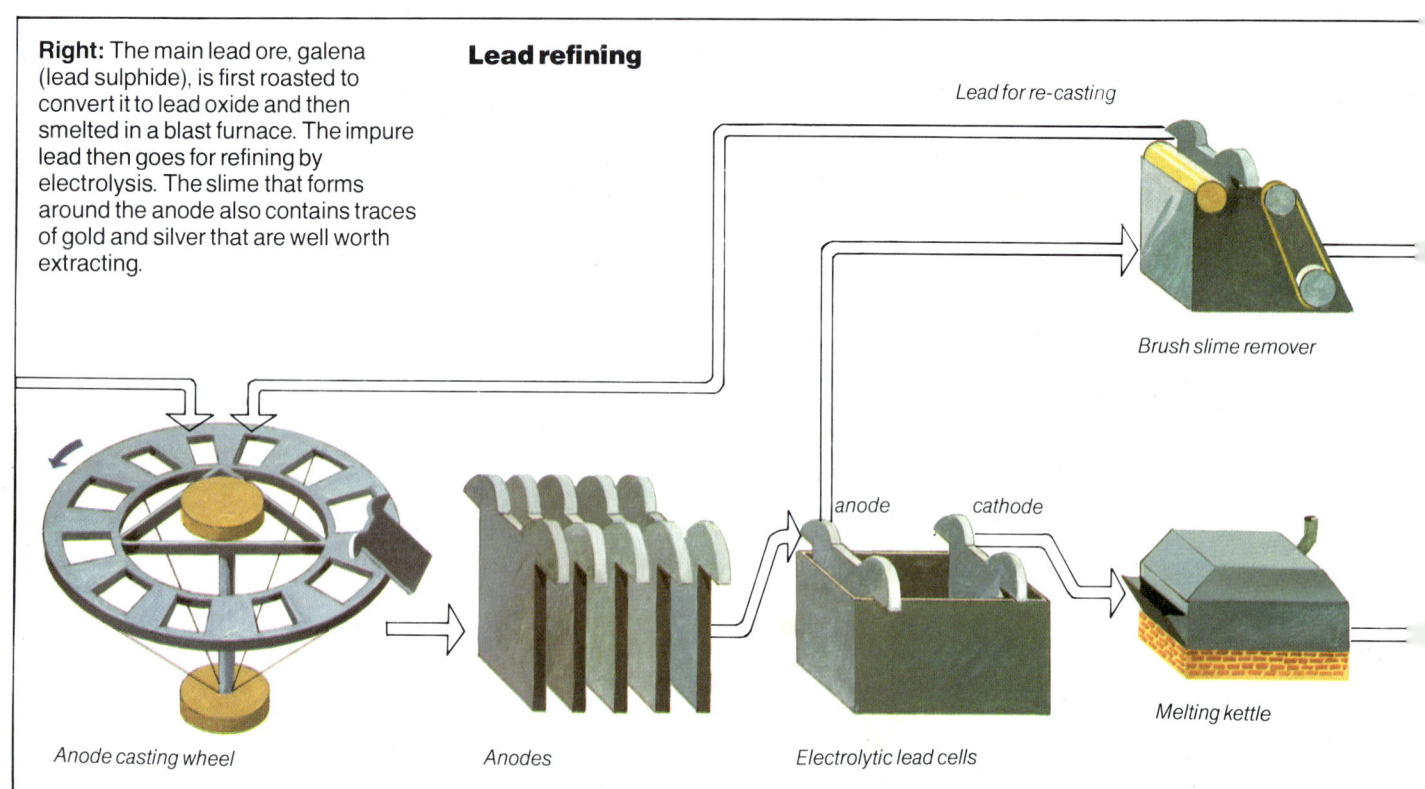

Right: The main lead ore, galena (lead sulphide), is first roasted to convert it to lead oxide and then smelted in a blast furnace. The impure lead then goes for refining by electrolysis. The slime that forms around the anode also contains traces of gold and silver that are well worth extracting.

Lead refining

Lead for re-casting

Brush slime remover

anode *cathode*

Melting kettle

Anode casting wheel *Anodes* *Electrolytic lead cells*

30

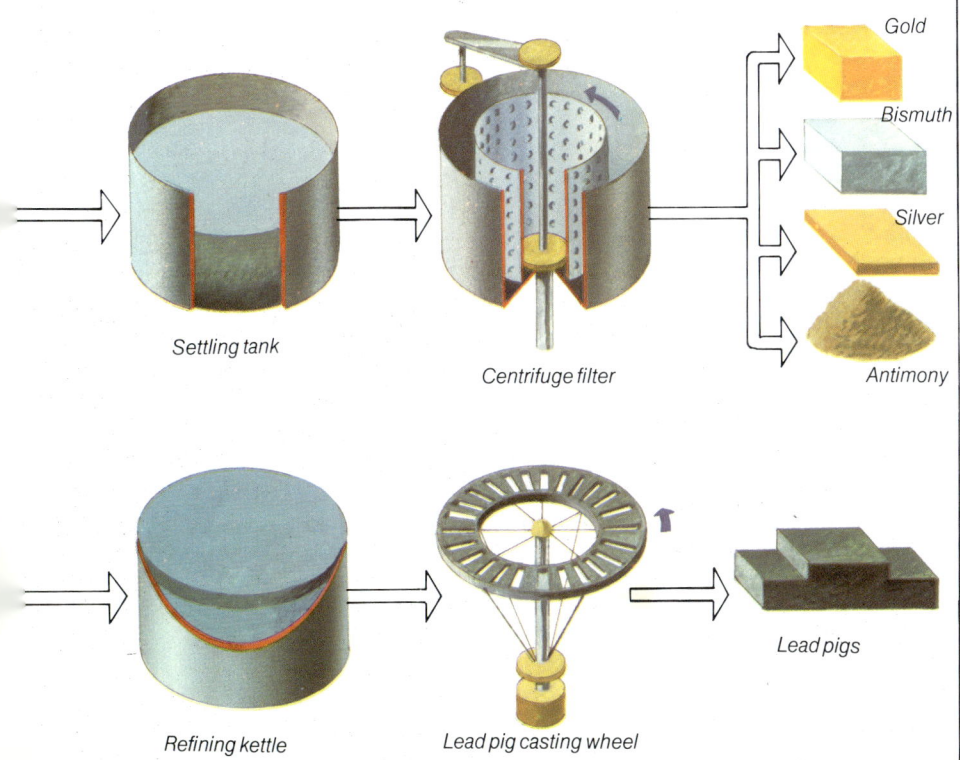

Settling tank
Centrifuge filter
Gold
Bismuth
Silver
Antimony
Refining kettle
Lead pig casting wheel
Lead pigs

the same amount of steel the basic-oxygen converter makes in just 40 minutes!

The electric-arc process differs from the others in that no hot metal is used, only steel scrap. Heat to melt the scrap is provided by an electric arc – a giant spark that jumps between the metal charge and huge carbon electrodes in the furnace roof. Lime and iron ore are added to the melted scrap to form a slag that absorbs impurities. This process is much cleaner and produces a higher grade steel.

Electrolytic refining

Electrolysis is used to refine copper, gold, silver, lead and nickel, and often follows initial fire refining. In refining copper, impure copper is made up into plates, which form the anodes in electrolytic cells. The cathodes are plates of pure copper. As electrolysis proceeds, copper gradually disappears from the anodes and is deposited, pure, on the cathodes. Impurities form a slime beneath the anodes.

Shaping hot metal

Continuous casting

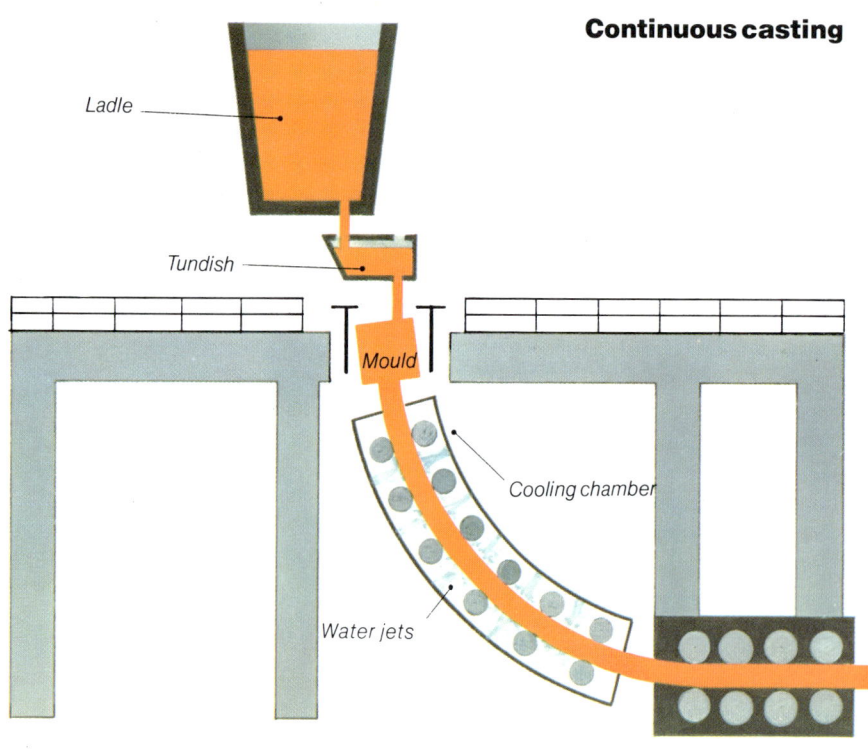

Left: Continuous casting produces slabs, billets and blooms directly from molten steel. The steel is poured from the ladle into the tundish, which is heated. From the tundish the steel flows steadily into a water-cooled mould, from which it is withdrawn via rollers as it solidifies. It is then cut to size.

Some metals, including copper, gold and silver, can readily be shaped when cold by bending and light hammering. They are very malleable.

Other metals, including steel, are much more difficult to shape when cold, for they are too hard and too strong. When they are red-hot, however, these metals become quite plastic and can then be shaped more easily by pressure (rolling mill), hammering (or forging), and extrusion (forcing through a die).

Casting

For a metal such as bronze, however, all these methods are unsuitable. The best way of shaping bronze is by casting – pouring the molten metal into a shaped mould so that when it cools, it takes the shape of the mould. A cast metal has a structure markedly different from that produced by the other shaping methods. In particular cast metal is brittle, which limits its uses. On the other hand, metals shaped by rolling, forging and extrusion, termed wrought metals, tend to be much stronger and tougher.

Casting takes place in a workshop called a foundry. The commonest form of casting uses sand moulds. A model of the object to be cast is placed in a box,

Below: A sand mould is usually made in two halves so that the model that forms in the shaped cavity can afterwards be withdrawn. The runner allows the metal to be poured in and the riser allows air inside to escape.

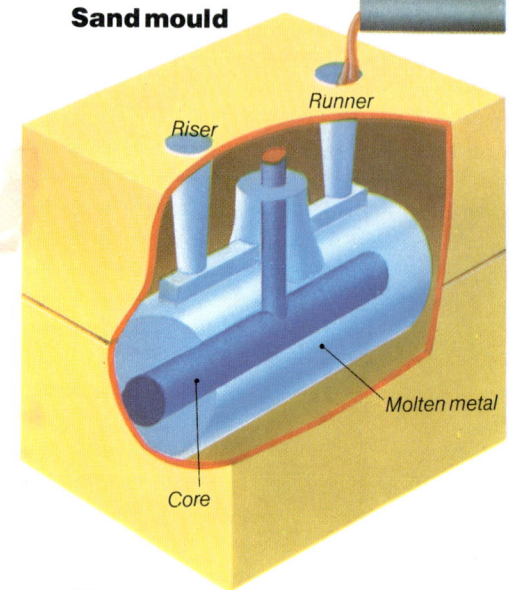

and a moist mixture of sand and clay is packed firmly around it. Channels are made in the top of the mould leading to the cavity inside. The molten metal is poured into one (called the runner), while the other (the riser) allows the air inside to escape as the metal fills the mould. When the metal has cooled and solidified, the mould is broken open and the casting released.

Some foundries employ permanent metal moulds, or dies, which can be used over and over again. Metal moulds are also used in pressure die-casting, an injection-moulding technique widely used for mass-producing small castings for toys and domestic appliances.

Rolling and forging

Many metals are also cast immediately after refining into a size and shape handy for other shaping operations. They may be cast either into individual ingots or into slabs on a continuous-casting machine.

The ingots or slabs are then reheated ready for rolling or forging. In rolling they are passed back and forth through pairs of heavy rollers, each set of rollers being called a stand. The distance between the rollers is progressively reduced, so that the metal gets thinner, longer and wider, like a lump of dough under a rolling pin. Depending on the profile of the rollers, the resulting product could be sheets, girders, bars, or rails.

In forging, the red-hot ingot or slab is pounded by a ram. In a drop forge the ram falls under gravity or is forced down onto the ingot by air or steam pressure. Usually the bed of the forge and the ram hold the two halves of a die, so that the metal is forced into shape when the two come together. In press forging the ram applies a progressive squeeze by means of hydraulic (liquid) pressure.

Left: This painting by Joseph Wright (1734-97) of Derby shows a traditional blacksmith at work in his forge. The blacksmith shapes red-hot iron by hammering it repeatedly on an anvil.

Right: Three stages in the casting of a ship's propeller. First the mould is prepared around a wooden model of the propeller (*top*). Then molten metal (usually a corrosion-resistant bronze) is poured into the completed mould (*centre*), from which the finished propeller is afterwards extracted (*bottom*).

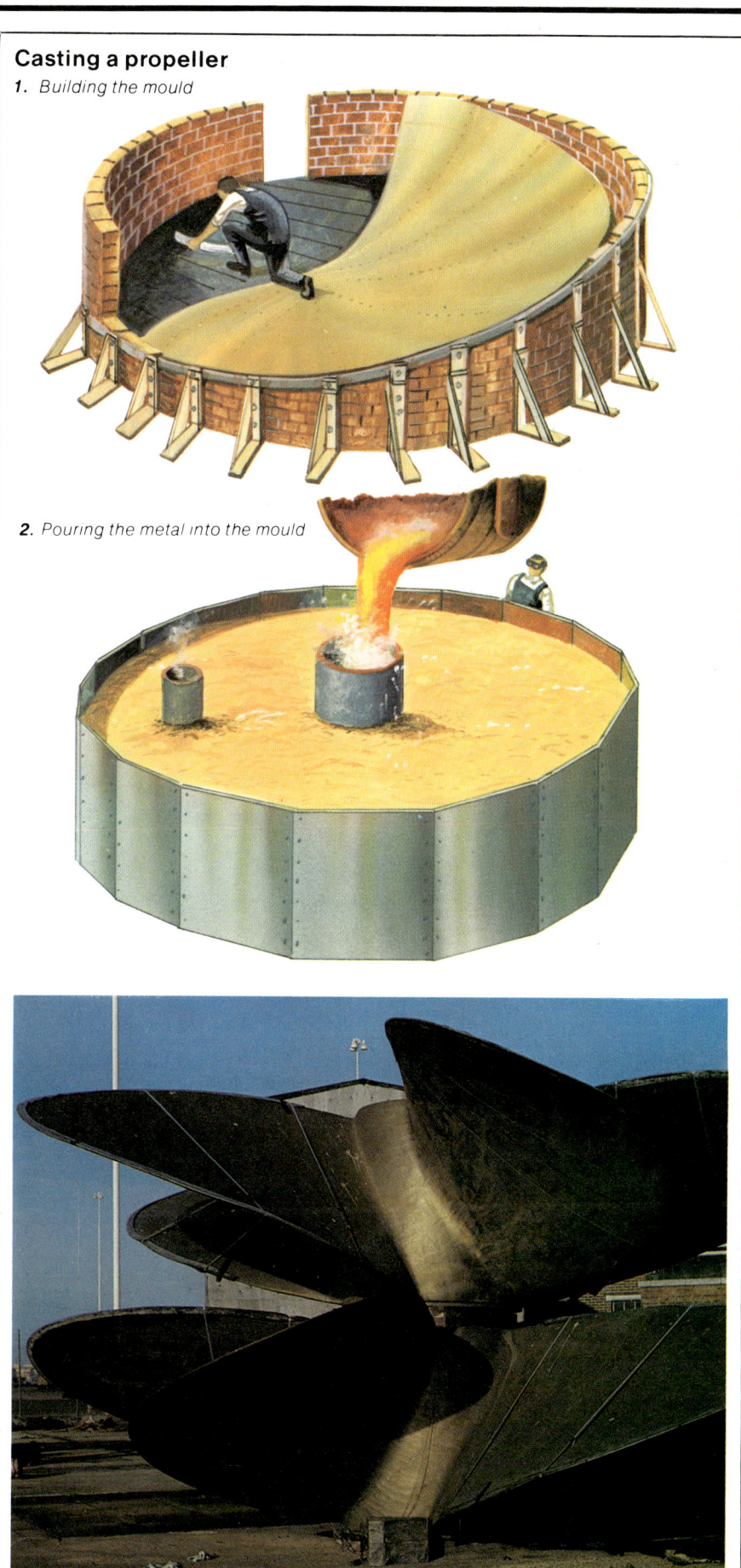

Casting a propeller
1. Building the mould

2. Pouring the metal into the mould

33

Shaping cold metal

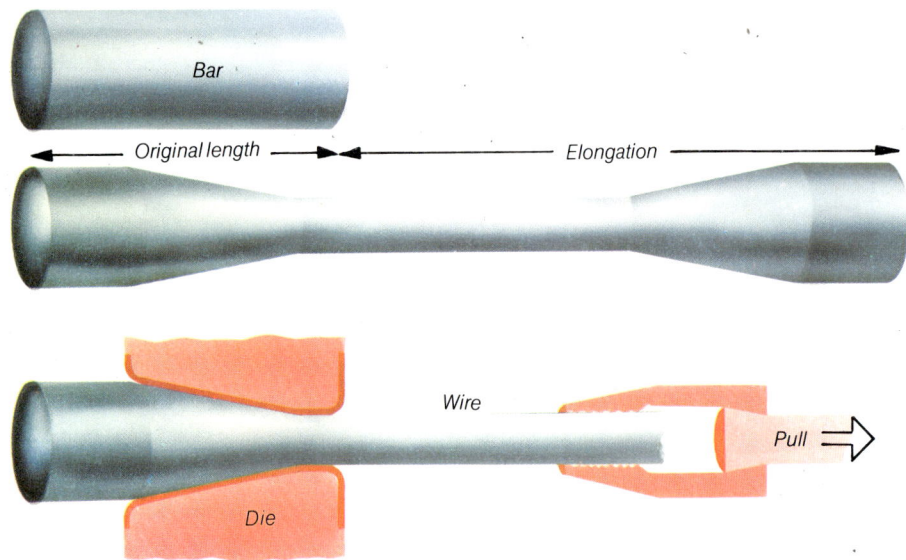

Above: Metals that are ductile can be drawn into wire by pulling them through a die. This diagram shows the general principle. In practice such a large reduction in diameter could not be achieved in one stage.

Below: Soft lead alloys can be made into flexible thin-walled tubes by impact extrusion. A slug of metal is struck by a ram, and the energy of impact makes the metal flow into and out of the die to form a tube shape.

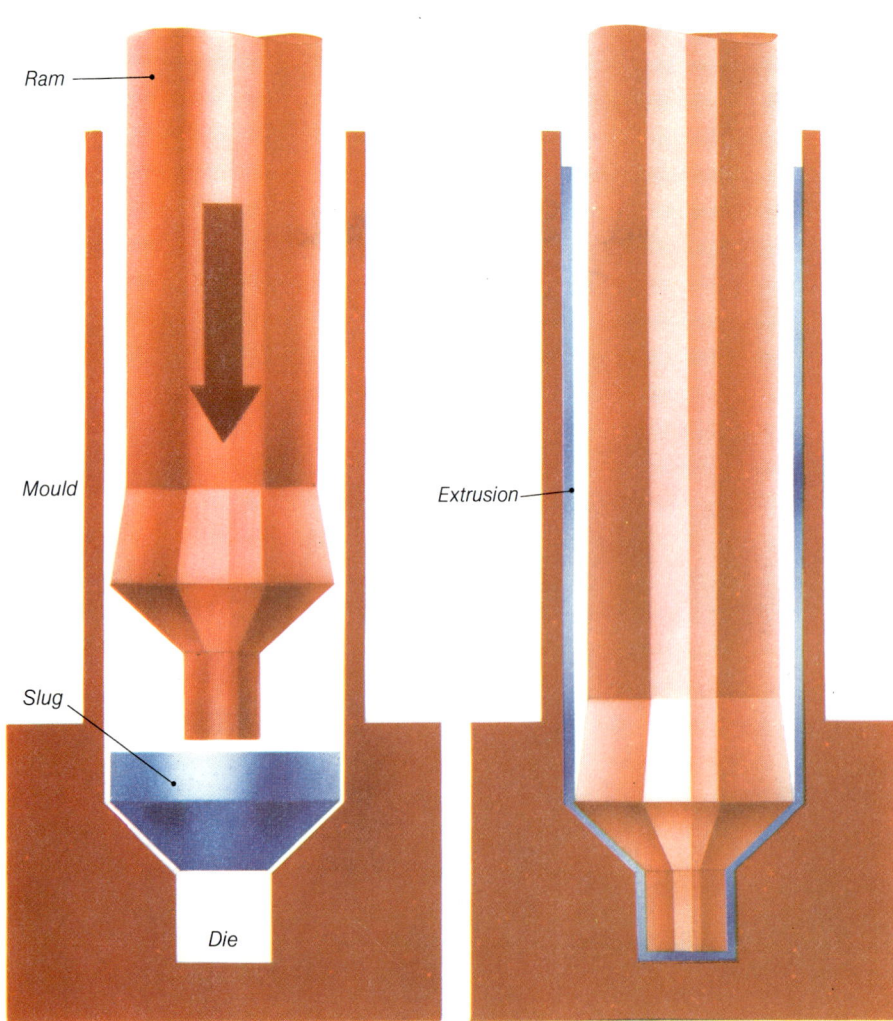

Rolling is a process used to shape not only hot metal, but also cold metal as well. In fact the sheet, strip and plate coming from the hot-rolling mills are often then cold rolled. Cold rolling carries out the final reduction in size and produces metal of accurate gauge (thickness) and with the desired surface finish.

Before cold rolling begins, the hot-rolled strip is pickled in acid. This treatment removes any oxide scale that has formed on the metal. The sheet then passes through several stands of rollers, but the reduction in size is quite small. Cold rolling, however, makes the metal very hard and stiff, and it then has to be heat treated to bring it back to a reasonable condition. It is first heated and then allowed to cool slowly – a treatment called annealing. A final light cold rolling follows annealing to give it the desired surface hardness and finish.

An alternative method of shaping sheet metal is called spinning. It is sometimes used, for example, to shape hollow metalware such as an aluminium teapot. The metal sheet is spun and a battery of rotating rollers are pressed against it to do the shaping of the object.

Pressing and stamping

A great deal of sheet steel produced by rolling goes to make car bodies. This sheet is cold pressed into body sections by hydraulic presses similar to those used for forging.

Buttons and coins are produced from sheet metal by cold stamping, which is really a small-scale version of drop forging. Circular blanks are punched out of the sheet, and then stamped with a pattern by being sandwiched between two dies.

A sudden blow is also used to shape soft metal alloys into collapsible tubes, such as those used for toothpaste. This method is known as impact extrusion. The metal is placed in a die. A sharp blow with a punch forces the metal to flow out of the die and around the outside of the punch, forming a thin-walled tube.

The sudden force caused by an explosion can also be used for shaping metals. The technique is known as explosive forming and the explosion forces the metal into a shaped die. It is often done underwater as this helps to contain the explosion and allow more control over the process.

Drawing

Drawing is another important method of shaping cold metal. It is used to produce wire from metal rods. Vast quantities of copper wire are required by the electrical industry, and steel wire also is much in demand for suspension bridge cables, springs and fencing.

In drawing, a metal rod is tapered and pulled through a die of slightly smaller diameter. The rod becomes narrower but longer. This process is continued a number of times through increasingly narrower dies until it becomes wire of the desired diameter. To resist wear, the dies are made from very hard tungsten carbide.

Copper wire drawing is comparatively easy, since copper is a very ductile metal. Steel is much tougher and must be reduced in size very gradually. Also, it must be annealed frequently to prevent it becoming too brittle and snapping.

Tubing, made by the extrusion of hot metal through a die, may also be cold drawn afterwards to give it accurate dimensions and a good surface finish.

Above: A cold sheet metal press is here shown in operation.

Below: A partly struck medal is placed between two dies prior to its final pressing.

Joining and cutting metal

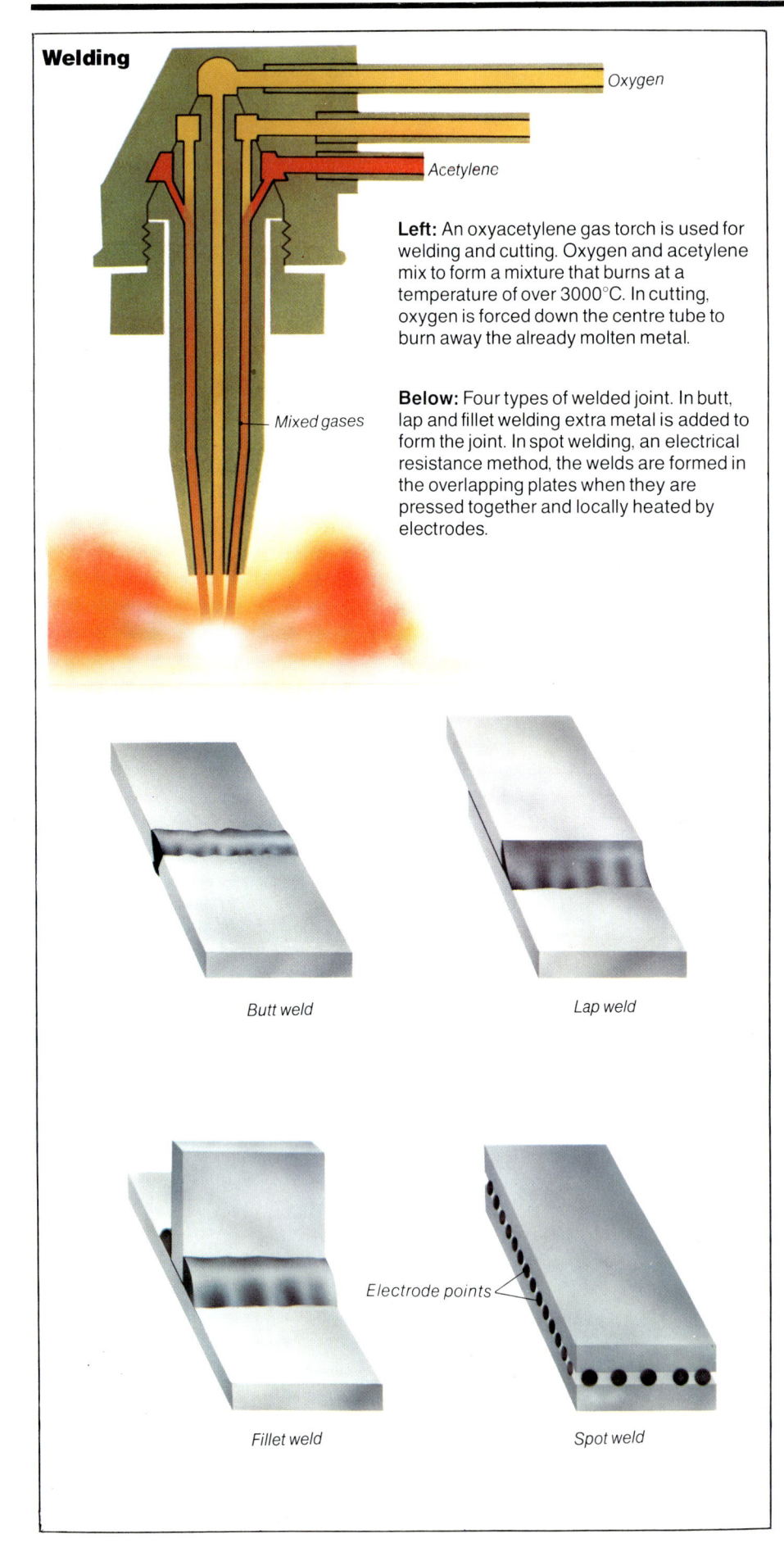

Welding

Left: An oxyacetylene gas torch is used for welding and cutting. Oxygen and acetylene mix to form a mixture that burns at a temperature of over 3000°C. In cutting, oxygen is forced down the centre tube to burn away the already molten metal.

Below: Four types of welded joint. In butt, lap and fillet welding extra metal is added to form the joint. In spot welding, an electrical resistance method, the welds are formed in the overlapping plates when they are pressed together and locally heated by electrodes.

Butt weld

Lap weld

Fillet weld

Spot weld

Many metal objects, including some large ones (such as ships' propellers), can be produced in one piece. But a great many more are so huge or so complicated that they have to be built up piece by piece.

For some uses the pieces can be joined simply by means of nuts and bolts. Holes drilled in the two pieces are lined up, the bolt is inserted and the nut screwed down on to it. Nuts can work loose, however, and a more permanent joint can be made by riveting.

Riveting
A rivet is a metal plug with a head at one end. It is inserted through the holes in overlapping plates so that the tail of the rivet protrudes. This is then hammered flat to form another head. The plates are sandwiched tightly between the two heads. Riveting is very widely used in aircraft construction and was once used to build ships' hulls.

Soldering and brazing
The mechanical methods of bolting and riveting are of little use for joining small pieces of metal, such as wires and tubes. Copper wires for electrical use and pipework for plumbing are joined together by soldering; steel tubing for bicycles by brazing; and steel plate for ships' hulls by welding.

All three processes involve the use of molten metal. Soldering uses an alloy of lead, tin and a little antimony, which melts at only about 200°C. The solder is applied to the metal joint with a soldering iron.

Brazing is so-called because it uses a brass for joining. Brass has a much higher melting point than solder – about 850°C – and forms a much stronger joint when it cools. The brass is melted into the joint from a filler rod heated by an oxyacetylene gas torch (so-called because it burns acetylene gas in oxygen).

Welding
The gas torch is also used in welding. Welding differs from the other processes in that the edges of the metal parts to be joined are heated red-hot. They then fuse (melt) together with the molten metal added from the filler rod. The resultant joint has a continuous internal structure that has great strength.

The heat to fuse the metal and melt the filler rod can also be provided by an electric arc – a continuous spark between two electrodes. Sometimes the filler rod is used as one electrode. Electric-arc welding is very much cleaner than gas welding, since no flames dirty the metal. It also lends itself to methods of keeping air away from the joint, as this could cause oxidation and hence weakness. In shielded arc welding an inert gas such as argon is delivered to the joint to keep the air away.

Another method of welding, resistance welding, also uses electricity. It is widely used in the car industry for automatically welding steel sheet. The sheets are overlapped, and a heavy current is passed between two electrodes touching each side. The electrical resistance of the metal between the joint causes it to heat up locally and fuse. Pressure is also applied to the joint at the same time. Thus both individual spot welds or continuous seam welds can be made.

Right: Soldering is normally carried out by means of a soldering 'iron', which is actually made of copper. A flux is used to clean the metal surface, preparing it to receive the solder.

Above left: Lasers can also be used for cutting and welding metals. This carbon dioxide laser is easily cutting through 3 mm thick alloy steel. The process is much more rapid and the accuracy much greater than with conventional methods.

Above: Riveting was once the main method of joining steel plates to form a ship's hull. Over 10 million rivets were used in the construction of the famous liner *Queen Mary*, now preserved as a floating hotel at Long Beach, California.

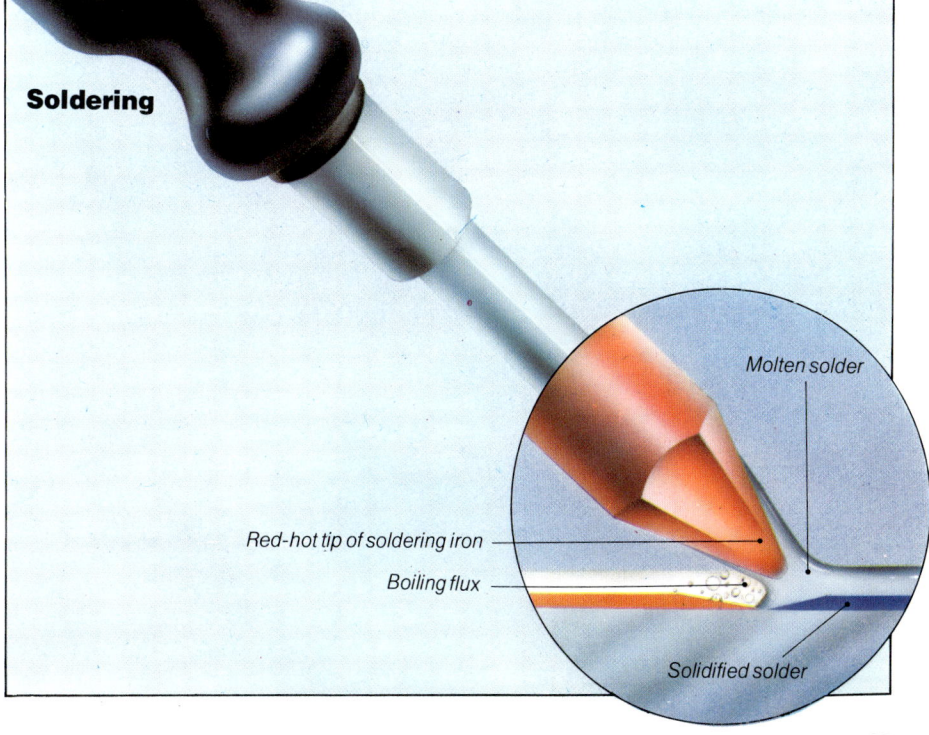

Soldering

Molten solder
Red-hot tip of soldering iron
Boiling flux
Solidified solder

Machining metal

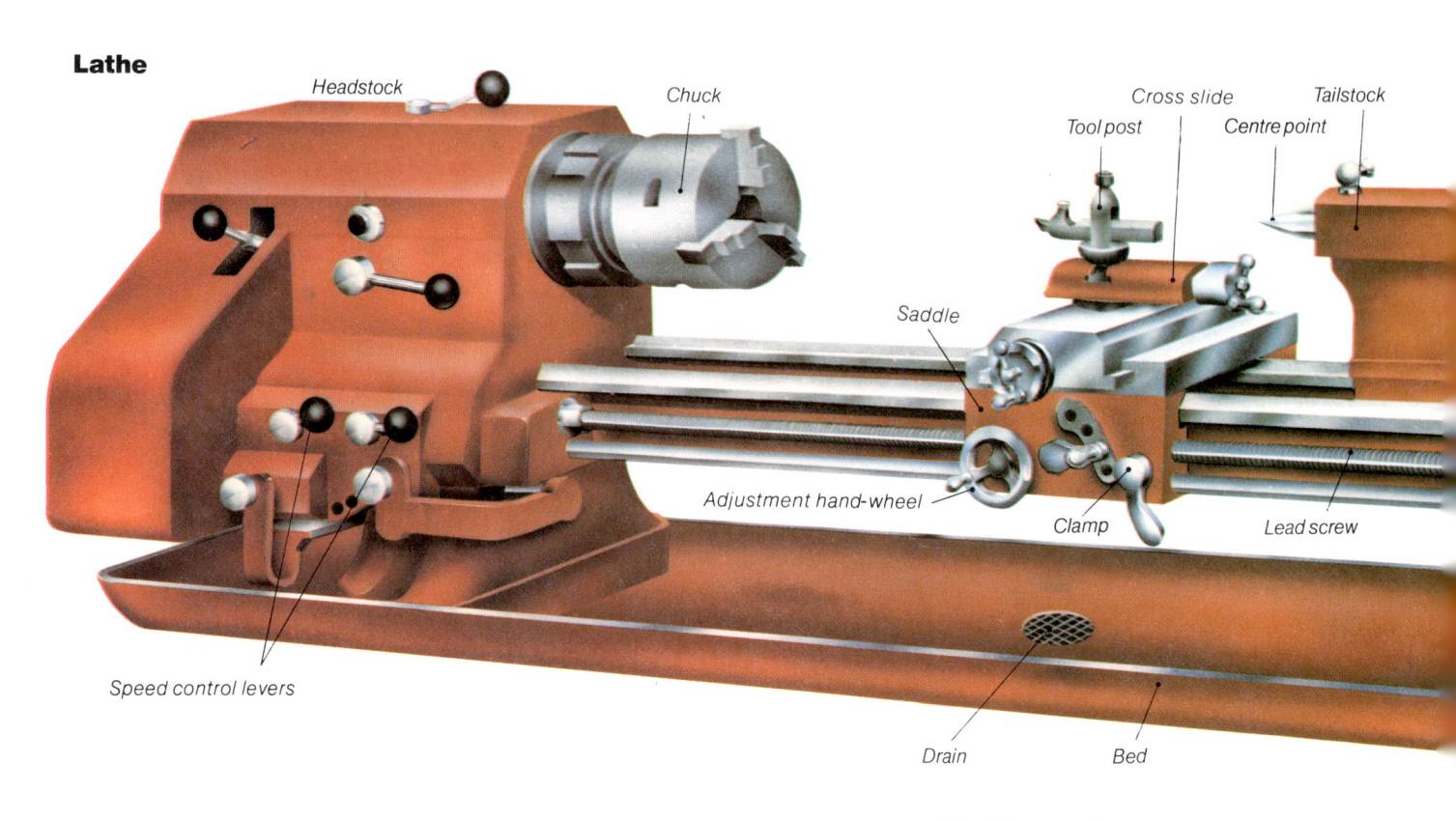

Lathe

Labels: Headstock, Chuck, Tool post, Cross slide, Tailstock, Centre point, Saddle, Adjustment hand-wheel, Clamp, Lead screw, Speed control levers, Drain, Bed

Above: The lathe is the most common and most useful machine tool found in engineering workshops. The workpiece is held in the chuck and rotated. It can be supported at the other end by the tailstock.

Below: This Herbert AL40 numerically-controlled lathe is one of the most advanced on the market. All the machining and repositioning operations take place automatically.

Although a piece of metal has been shaped by casting, forging or some other process, it often requires further trimming, drilling, or other treatment to complete the shaping process. For example, a cast-iron car engine block needs many holes drilled through it to take bolts, and the cylinders must be very accurately bored to take the pistons.

Machine tools

Finishing treatments which involve the cutting of some metal from the object are termed machining, and are carried out by machine tools. Machine tools play a vital role in mass production processes because they work to very accurate limits and can turn out identical parts every time.

All machine tools have a means of firmly clamping the workpiece – the object to be machined. They have a means of moving the cutting tool into the workpiece, or of moving the workpiece past the tool, or of doing both. They have powerful motors to make the tool cut through the metal, which is machined cold.

Cutting processes

The cutting tools themselves have to be very sharp and hard enough to keep their sharpness during machining. Special high-speed tool steels containing tungsten and chromium are generally used. They retain their strength and cutting edge even when running red-hot.

In many machining operations a light oil-and-water emulsion is directed at the cutting area. This serves both to lubricate and to cool both the workpiece and tool, which naturally heat up due to the effect of friction.

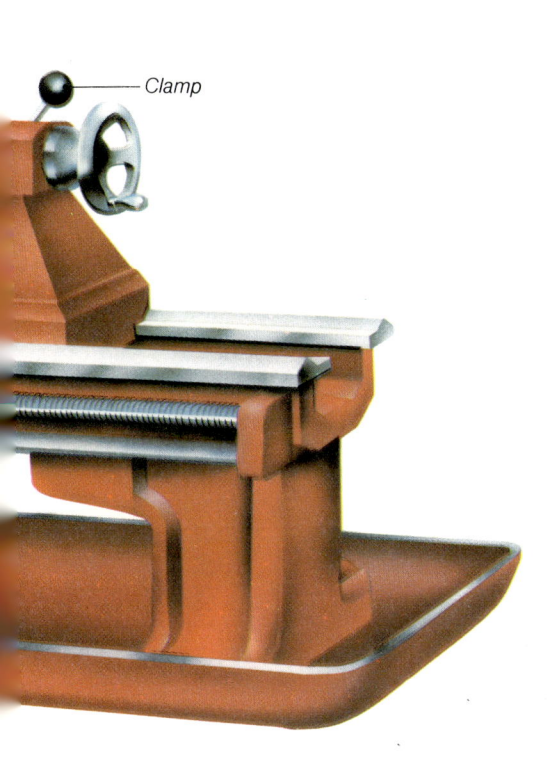

The most common of all machine tools is the lathe. It is typically used to machine shafts and cylinders, which are clamped in a chuck and rotated horizontally. The machining process on a lathe is called turning.

Drilling is another common machining operation carried out on a drill press. It is done by a rotating drill bit, which is lowered vertically into the workpiece. The bit cuts only at the tip, and has spiral grooves cut along it to allow the swarf to escape. In boring and reaming different kinds of tools are used to enlarge a hole already drilled.

In milling, the cutting tool is a rotating toothed wheel, which remains fixed while the workpiece moves beneath it. In grinding, metal is removed gradually by contact with a spinning abrasive wheel.

Automation

With ordinary machine tools a human operator is required to switch on, select the tool and tool speed, and position and reposition the tool and workpiece during machining. With some new machines all the operator needs to do is switch on. These numerically controlled machines follow coded instructions fed to them from magnetic tape.

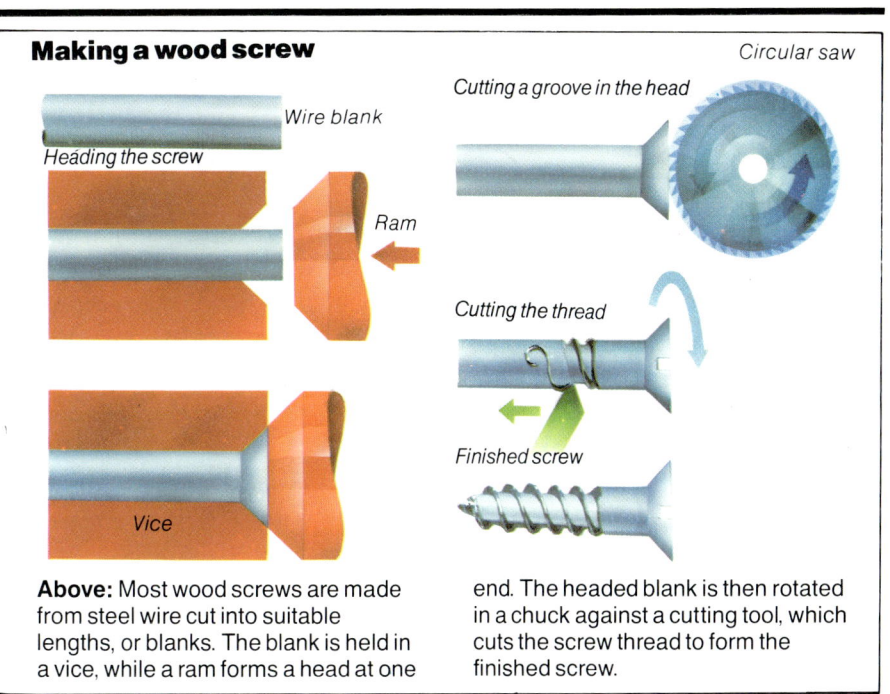

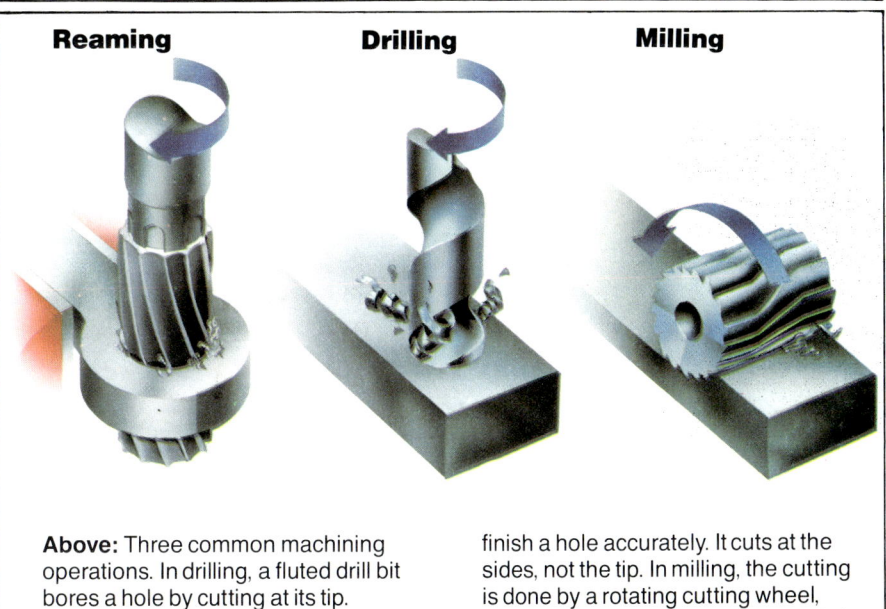

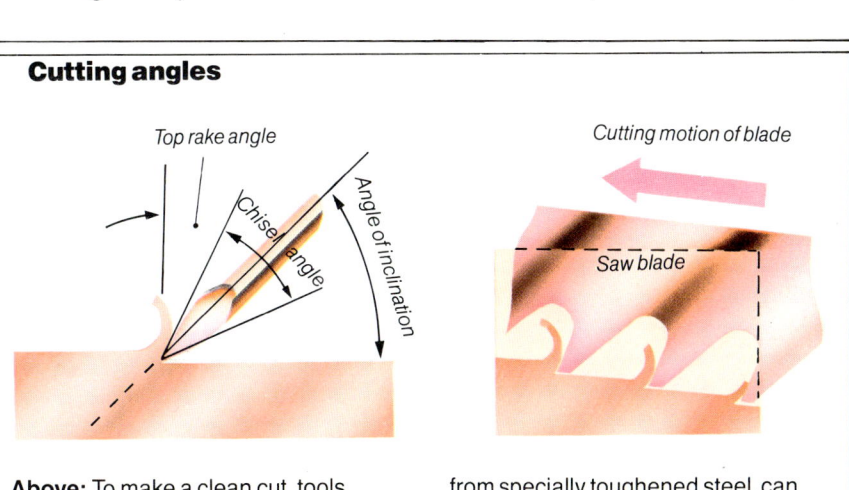

Making a wood screw

Above: Most wood screws are made from steel wire cut into suitable lengths, or blanks. The blank is held in a vice, while a ram forms a head at one end. The headed blank is then rotated in a chuck against a cutting tool, which cuts the screw thread to form the finished screw.

Reaming   Drilling   Milling

Above: Three common machining operations. In drilling, a fluted drill bit bores a hole by cutting at its tip. Reaming uses a parallel-sided bit to finish a hole accurately. It cuts at the sides, not the tip. In milling, the cutting is done by a rotating cutting wheel, while the workpiece moves beneath it.

Cutting angles

Above: To make a clean cut, tools must be tapered and set at the correct cutting angles. A metal saw, made from specially toughened steel, can cut through metal easily if its teeth are set at the proper angle.

39

Decorative metalwork

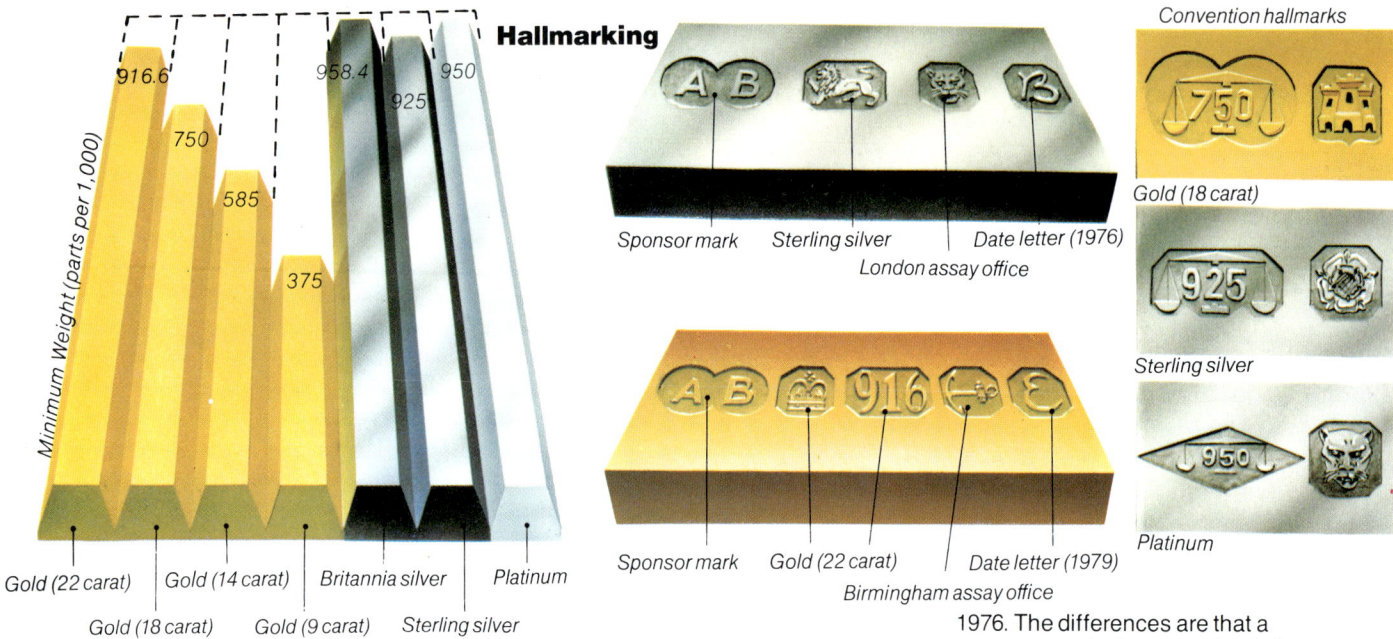

Hallmarking

Minimum Weight (parts per 1,000)

916.6, 750, 585, 375, 958.4, 925, 950

Gold (22 carat), Gold (18 carat), Gold (14 carat), Gold (9 carat), Britannia silver, Sterling silver, Platinum

Sponsor mark — Sterling silver — Date letter (1976)
London assay office

Sponsor mark — Gold (22 carat) — Date letter (1979)
Birmingham assay office

Convention hallmarks

Gold (18 carat)

Sterling silver

Platinum

Above: Hallmarking gold and silver articles dates back to 1300 in the UK. A hallmark is proof that the metal used conforms to legal standards of fineness or purity. The sponsor mark indicates the manufacturer, the standard mark shows the precious metal content, the assay office mark identifies where it was tested, and the date letter shows the year.

Convention hallmarks are international marks approved only in 1976. The differences are that a common control mark replaces the standard mark, and there is no date letter.

Any other marks on precious metals have been struck by the manufacturer and are unlikely to have been independently tested.

Most of this book is concerned with the properties and production of metals that are of practical use to us. But metals can also be fashioned and decorated by craftsmen into fine works of art. This has happened from the very beginnings of metalworking, more than 7,000 years ago.

The early metalworkers worked with the native metals copper, gold and silver. These metals are still widely used by craftsmen today and for much the same reasons. They are attractive to look at, do not corrode easily and are easy to work. They can be bent, hammered, drawn into wire and cut with ease.

The first man-made metal – the alloy bronze – cannot be worked in this way because it is too brittle, but it can readily be cast into shaped moulds. Fine bronzes have been produced by different civilizations. The Renaissance sculptures of Ghiberti and Donatello perhaps show this art form at its finest. Other alloys, such as brass and pewter, have similar properties and have long been used for making decorative objects. Iron has also been cast for ornamentation, but usually for architectural purposes. A fine example is provided by many of the iron balconies in the French Quarter of New Orleans.

Techniques

Hammering techniques include forging and embossing. Forging is used for shaping wrought iron and involves beating the red-hot iron with a heavy hammer on an anvil. This is the traditional blacksmith's craft. Embossing, practised on the softer metals, involves hammering to produce a raised design. The piece of metal is beaten on the reverse side, so that the raised pattern appears on the face. This decorative method is also called *repoussé*.

Designs may be cut into the metal face in a number of ways. They may be cut deeply by chasing, using a hammer and small chisel-like tools. Alternatively, they may be cut more delicately by engraving, using sharp hand tools. Some metals, including copper and pewter, have designs etched in them with acid. They are first covered in wax,

Left: This piece of jewellery, called 'Ecstasy', was designed by Jacqueline Mina in 18 carat gold and carved, frosted rock crystal encrusted with diamonds and tourmalines.

into which a pattern is scratched. They are then dipped in acid which attacks and dissolves away the metal exposed by the scratching.

Enamelling and gilding are among many other decorative techniques. In enamelling, hollows made in the metal surface are filled with coloured enamel paints. Gilding uses the unsurpassed ability of gold to be beaten into very thin sheet, or leaf – as thin as 0.000001 of a millimetre thick. It involves applying the gold leaf to other metals, plaster, glass and even wood.

Above: Silver is an easy metal to shape by hand, being relatively soft and ductile. Here a Thai silversmith is decorating silverware by embossing.

Below: The decorative iron balconies in the French Quarter of New Orleans were erected mainly in the 19th century. The earliest examples were fashioned in wrought iron, the later ones in cast iron.

Metals tomorrow

Below: Modern high-speed multi-role jets like Panavia's *Tornado* demand high-performance materials that will retain their strength at high temperatures. Superalloys containing nickel, chromium, titanium and tungsten are used in the jet's engines.

Below: Metals that can withstand searing temperatures are also essential in rockets. This picture, taken at the Johnson Space Centre at Houston, Texas, shows the booster engines of a Saturn V moon rocket in front of a Mercury-Redstone rocket.

The mineral ore deposits from which we obtain our metals have formed over periods of hundreds of millions of years. It was once thought that they were too large ever to run out. But in just a few generations man has come close to exhausting many of them. Within a few decades the position will become very serious indeed, and there will be a shortage of many metals vital to our present civilization, including gold, silver, copper, uranium, platinum, tungsten and lead. Fortunately, there are ample supplies of our two most important metals – iron and aluminium – enough to last us for several centuries.

Prospecting

To put off the evil day when the metals run out, geologists are energetically searching far and wide for new mineral deposits. They are using satellite photographs to prospect for deposits on land, and are boring and dredging to find deposits offshore.

In fact on, rather than in, the seabed they have found what could be an answer to many of the world's metal supply problems. In the deep ocean there occur lumps, or nodules, rich in manganese, copper, nickel, cobalt and other metals. And, geologically speaking, they are forming at a rapid rate, maybe even as fast as we use the metals they contain. The nodules are going to be difficult to mine, but several plans have already been put forward.

Above: Where precision and a clean weld are required, welding may be done by means of electron beams.

Alternatives

Another approach to the impending shortage of metals is recycling. This means re-using the same metal over and over again. Instead of throwing metal products away after use, they are collected and resmelted. A certain amount of recycling has always been practised, especially with precious metals. But in tomorrow's world it must become the rule for all metals.

A different method of tackling the problem is to find materials that will do the same job as metals. Here plastic materials often prove successful. Car bodies and boat hulls can now be built in glass-reinforced plastic (GRP), commonly known as fibreglass. It is strong and tough and, unlike the sheet steel it replaces, does not rust. Fibreglass is only one of several composite materials now in use. Another, based on carbon fibres, is strong enough to be used in aircraft structures.

Space age

Far-sighted observers claim that we may one day be mining the Moon for metals. They would not be used back here on Earth, but rather for building manned stations and colonies out in space. It is also possible that in the nearer future many metals will be smelted and fabricated in space. Under the vacuum and zero gravity conditions of space, purer and stronger metals could be produced, as demonstrated by the Skylab astronauts in 1973-74.

Perfect metal crystals can be grown in space. These could then be used as reinforcement for other metals. Experiments in this technique, using carefully grown fibre-like metal crystals, have already produced spectacular results. Crystal-reinforcement can often double the strength of the base metal.

The high technology of the world tomorrow will demand super-metals like this. It will also demand new methods of fabrication which will result in a more accurate and purer product. These methods will include such advanced techniques as electron-beam welding, laser cutting, and electrochemical machining – all of which are already past the experimental stage.

Above: The massive space structures that will feature in tomorrow's world will be built in orbit with the help of this beam builder. This NASA-developed machine automatically fabricates triangular aluminium beams from sheet metal coils.
Below: Though there is still plenty of aluminium left in the ground, extraction is increasingly expensive since it requires vast amounts of electricity. Aluminium for recycling is collected here.

A-Z glossary

Actinides are a group of heavy radioactive metals. These include the naturally occurring actinium (Ac), thorium (Th), protactinium (Pa) and uranium (U), together with the artificial elements neptunium (Np), plutonium (Pu), Americium (Am), curium (Cm), berkelium (Bk), californium (Cf), einsteinium (Es), fermium (Fm), mendelevium (Md), nobelium (No) and lawrencium (Lr).
Age hardening is a property of some alloys, particularly of aluminium, that enables the metal to harden several days after undergoing heat treatment.
Alkali metals are metals such as sodium and potassium which form strongly alkaline solutions in water.
Alkaline-earth metals are metals such as calcium and magnesium which form mildly alkaline solutions in water.
Alnico is an alloy of aluminium, nickel and cobalt used to make powerful permanent magnets.
Aluminium (Al) is the commonest lightweight metal, mostly used in the form of alloys. Its main ore is bauxite.
Amalgam is an alloy of mercury with another metal.
Annealing is a method of heat treatment in which a metal is heated and allowed to cool slowly.
Anodizing is a method of increasing the thickness of the protective oxide film on aluminium.
Antimony (Sb) is a brittle metal used as a hardener in alloys, such as type metal. Its main ore is stibnite.

Babbit metal is an alloy used for bearings, containing tin, copper, antimony and sometimes lead.
Barium (Ba) is a soft alkaline-earth metal whose compounds are used to colour fireworks. Its main ore is barytes.
Beryllium (Be) is a very light alkaline-earth metal used in alloys for airframes. Its main ore is beryl.
Bismuth (Bi) is a brittle metal resembling antimony, used in easy melting, fusible alloys. Its main ore is bismuthite.
Brass is an alloy of copper and zinc.
Bronze is an alloy containing copper and tin, though some so-called bronzes contain no tin.

Cadmium (Cd) is a soft metal related to zinc, used for electroplating and in nuclear reactor control rods. Its main ore is greenockite.
Caesium (Cs) is a rare alkali metal, used as a vapour in atomic clocks.
Calcium (Ca) is a soft alkaline-earth metal, seldom used in the metallic state.
Carburizing is heating steel in contact with carbon to increase its hardness; also called case hardening.
Cermet is a combination of a ceramic material and a metal which resists high temperatures.

Chromium (Cr) is a very hard metal widely used for electroplating and in many corrosion- and heat-resistant alloys. Its main ore is chromite.
Cobalt (Co) is a tough metal widely used in magnetic alloys. It is mostly obtained as a by-product from copper ores.
Copper (Cu) is an attractive reddish metal which can be found native. It is a very good conductor, and resists corrosion.
Creep is the tendency of a metal to deform gradually under a constant load.
Cupronickel is a silvery alloy of copper and nickel used widely to make 'silver' coins.

Dendrite is the tree-like crystal form of some metals.
Ductility is the ease with which a metal can be deformed, for example, drawn into wire.
Duralumin is a strong, light alloy containing mainly aluminium and copper. It shows age hardening.

Elastic limit is the maximum stress a metal can withstand before being permanently stretched.
Electrolysis is the splitting-up by electricity of a compound in solution or when molten.

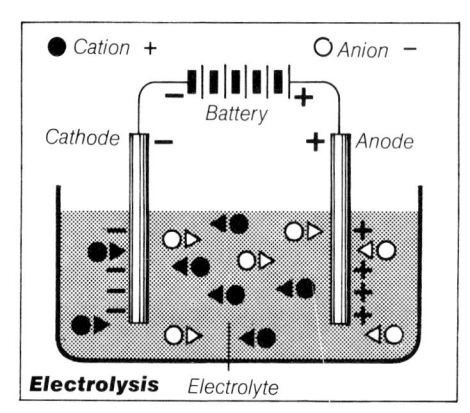

Electrolysis

Ferrous metals include iron and alloys that contain iron.
Flotation is a method of mineral dressing that uses a floating froth to separate mineral particles from an ore (see picture).

Gallium (Ga) is a rare soft metal that resembles aluminium.
Gangue is unwanted rocky or earthy material mined with an ore.

Germanium (Ge) is a rare metal with a pronounced crystalline structure. It is used as a semiconductor.
Gold (Au) is an attractive and durable precious metal. It is more ductile and malleable than any other. It is found native and as traces in many ores.
Gun metal is a corrosion-resistant alloy of copper, tin and zinc.

Hafnium (Hf) is a rare metal that resembles titanium. It is used in nuclear reactor control rods.
Heat treatment is the controlled heating and cooling of metals to produce more favourable physical properties.
Hooke's law states that in a metal, stress goes in proportion to strain up to the elastic limit.

Indium (In) is a rare soft metal, mostly used in semiconductors.
Invar is a nickel-iron alloy that scarcely expands or contracts at all with temperature changes.
Iron (Fe) is a very abundant magnetic metal used mostly in alloys.

Lead (Pb) is a soft, heavy metal, used in many alloys and in car batteries. Its main ore is galena.
Lithium (Li) is the lightest metal. It is related to sodium, but rarely used.

Magnesium (Mg) is a light alkaline-earth metal used in aircraft alloys.
Malleability is a property of a metal that allows it to be hammered or otherwise deformed without breaking.
Manganese (Mn) is a hard metal used mostly to toughen steels. Its main ore is pyrolusite. It occurs in nodules on the sea bed (see picture).

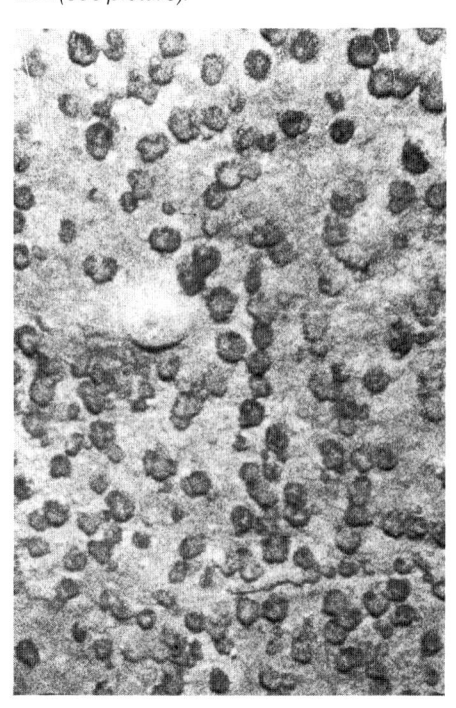

Mercury (Hg) is the only metal that is liquid at room temperature. Its nickname is quicksilver. It is used in barometers and thermometers and as silver and gold amalgams for teeth fillings; the main ore is cinnabar.
Metalloid is an element that has some properties of a metal, but others of a non-metal. Examples are arsenic, boron and germanium.
Mild steel is the commonest form of steel, containing up to about 0.25% carbon.
Mineral dressing is concentrating an ore before smelting.
Molybdenum (Mo) is a strong, hard metal with a high melting point, used in cutting steels. Its main ore is molybdenite.
Monel is a natural copper-nickel alloy obtained by smelting Sudbury (Canada) ore.

Nickel (Ni) is a tough, hard metal, used in electroplating and in a host of alloys, particularly with copper. Its main ore is pentlandite.
Nickel silver is an alloy of copper, zinc and nickel widely used as a base for electroplating. It is also called German silver.
Nimonic alloys are high-temperature alloys containing mainly nickel and chromium, widely used in jet engines.
Niobium (Nb) is a rare temperature-resistant metal, used in alloys for jet engines and missiles.
Non-ferrous metals are metals other than iron, or alloys containing no iron.

Osmium (Os) is the heaviest of all metals, related to platinum and equally rare.

Pewter is an alloy of tin and lead.
Platinum (Pt) is a rare precious metal, used in jewellery and as a catalyst in the chemical industry.
Platinum group are rare metals, often occurring naturally with platinum and possessing similar properties. They include palladium (Pd), rhodium (Rh), ruthenium (Ru), osmium (Os) and iridium (Ir).
Potassium (K) is a soft alkali metal, seldom used in a metallic form.
Powder metallurgy is a method of shaping metals, such as platinum and tungsten, with high melting points. The powdered metal is pressed into a mould and then sintered (heated strongly).

Quenching is plunging a hot metal into water or oil as part of heat treatment.

Radium (Ra) is a very rare radioactive metal, whose radiation is used to treat cancer. It occurs in pitchblende.
Rare earths are a group of rare metals with similar properties which occur together, commonly in the mineral monazite. Also called lanthanides, they include lanthanum (La), cerium (Ce), praseodymium (Pr), neodymium (Nd), promethium (Pr), samarium (Sm), europium (Eu), gadolinium (Gd), terbium (Tb), dysprosium (Dy), holmium (Ho), erbium (Er), thulium (Tm), ytterbium (Yb) and lutetium (Lu).
Refractory materials such as silica and alumina are chiefly used in brick form for lining enclosed areas that experience very high temperatures, e.g. a furnace. They resist change at high temperatures.
Rhenium (Re) is a rare metal with a high melting point; little used.
Rubidium (Rb) is an alkali metal; little used.

Silver (Ag) is a precious metal which has better conductivity than any other. It is used in jewellery and for electroplating.
Sodium is a soft, reactive alkali metal that is used molten as a coolant in some nuclear reactors.
Solder is a low-melting-point alloy containing tin and lead, widely used to join electrical wires and plumbing joints.
Strain is the amount of elongation, or stretch, produced when a material is stressed.
Stress is the load imposed on a unit area of a material.
Strontium (Sr) is an alkaline-earth metal resembling calcium whose compounds are used to colour fireworks.

Tantalum (Ta) is a rare metal sometimes used in high-temperature alloys. It was once called columbium.
Tempering is warming a metal after it has been quenched, to reduce its hardness.
Thallium (Tl) is a soft metal related to lead; little used.
Thermit process is a method of producing molten iron by burning a mixture of powdered iron oxide and aluminium.
Thorium (Th) is a heavy radioactive metal used in the nuclear industry. It occurs in monazite and thorite.
Tin (Sn) is a soft metal that resists corrosion, widely used in alloys and as a coating on steel (tinplate). Its main ore is cassiterite.
Titanium (Ti) is a strong, light and corrosion-resistant metal used in aircraft construction. Its main ore is rutile.

Transition metals are groups of metals with broadly similar properties which occur side by side in the periodic table. The first group, which includes titanium, vanadium, chromium, manganese, iron, cobalt, nickel and copper, is by far the most important in metallurgy.
Transuranium metals are man-made metals beyond uranium in the periodic table of elements.
Tungsten (W) is the metal that has the highest melting point. It is used as the filament in light bulbs and in high-temperature alloys. Its main ore is scheelite.
Type metal is an alloy of lead, tin and antimony, used for casting type.

Uranium (U) is a rare radioactive metal used as 'fuel' in nuclear reactors. Its main ore is pitchblende.

Vanadium (V) is a relatively rare, hard metal used to strengthen steels.

Wood's metal is an alloy of bismuth, lead, tin and cadmium that melts at the low temperature of 70°C. It is used to plug fire sprinkler systems.

Zinc (Zn) is a soft, corrosion-resistant metal used in many alloys, including brass, and for coating (galvanizing) steel. Its main ore is zinc blende.
Zirconium (Zr) is a rare soft metal which ignites easily. It is used in flashbulbs and in nuclear reactors because it absorbs few neutrons.

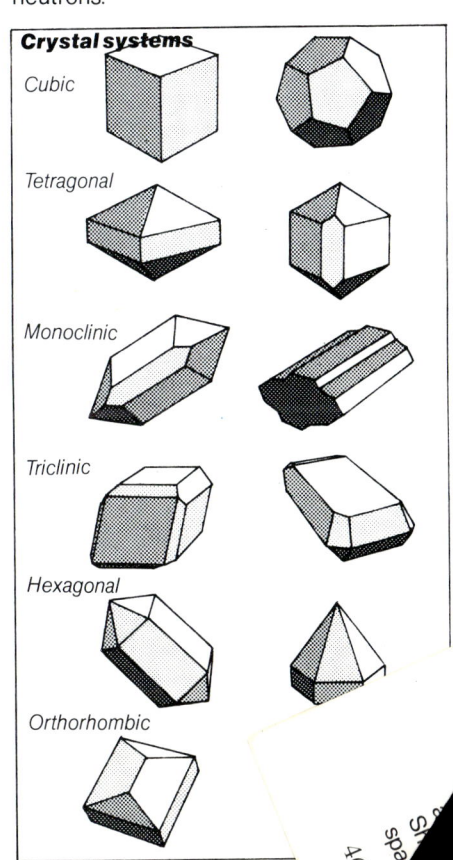

Crystal systems

Cubic

Tetragonal

Monoclinic

Triclinic

Hexagonal

Orthorhombic

Reference

Milestones in metal history

Before 4000 BC. Copper, gold, and iron from meteorites are hammered into ornaments and occasionally tools.
c. 4000 BC. Copper is smelted from its ores and used for casting in moulds. Native silver is also used.
c. 3500 BC. Mixed ores of copper and tin are smelted in Mesopotamia to produce bronze.
c. 3000 BC. 'Lost-wax' process is used for making intricate castings. Tin is smelted. Soldering is practised.
c. 1500 BC. Hittites begin smelting iron on a large scale in Anatolia (modern Turkey). The process yields a spongy iron, which we would call now wrought iron.
c. 1000 BC. Hard steel implements are being made by reheating spongy iron in contact with charcoal and then quenching in water.
c. 600 BC. The Chinese begin smelting iron in a superior furnace and produce molten metal, which can then be cast. Melting is possible because the high phosphorus content of the ore used makes the resultant iron melt more easily.
c. 200 BC. The Romans establish a thriving brass industry, using the alloy on a large scale for the first time.
c. 100 BC. Mercury is distilled from its ores. Amalgamation — treatment with mercury to form an amalgam — is used to extract gold from ores.

0–700 AD. Alchemists, in trying to transmute base metals into gold, thoroughly investigate the properties of metals and their compounds, laying the foundations for modern chemistry and metallurgy.
c. 700 AD. Iron-makers in Catalonia, Spain, develop a superior iron-smelting furnace, now known as the Catalan forge.
1300s. The prototype blast furnace came into use in Europe. In this shaft-type furnace the iron remains in contact with the charcoal for a longer time. It absorbs more carbon, which lowers its melting point to below the temperature of the furnace. The furnace thus produces molten iron which can be cast.
1600s. Tinplating — coating iron with a layer of tin — begins in Bohemia (now Czechoslovakia).
1709. English iron-master Abraham Darby introduces coke for iron smelting, replacing charcoal which is becoming scarce in England. Bigger furnaces result because coke is stronger than charcoal and can support a bigger charge of iron ore.
1740. English clockmaker Benjamin Huntsman invents the crucible process for making steel. English metallurgist William Champion develops zinc smelting.
1779. Abraham Darby, grandson of the iron-master mentioned above (1709), completes a cast-iron bridge at Coalbrookdale, Shropshire. The first iron bridge, with a span of 43 metres, it was used by traffic continuously until the 1950s.
1784. English iron-maker Henry Cort develops the 'puddling' process for converting pig iron into wrought iron — by heating pig iron with iron ore and stirring it with a ladle.
1807-8. English chemist Humphry Davy develops electrolysis process for isolating metals from their molten compounds. He isolates sodium, potassium, calcium, magnesium and barium.
1825. Danish scientist Hans Christian Oersted discovers aluminum.
1828. Scottish engineer James Neilson uses a hot-air blast in the blast furnace, and greatly reduces fuel consumption.
1839. American inventor Isaac Babbitt develops babbit metal — a tin, antimony and copper alloy suitable for machine bearings. English engineer James Nasmyth invents the steam hammer, which begins to supersede the water-driven tilt hammer previously used for working iron.
1856. English inventor Henry Bessemer introduces his converter process for producing steel cheaply, by blowing air through molten pig iron.
1864. French steelmakers Pierre and Emile Martin build the first open-hearth furnace. It incorporates regenerators, or air preheaters, invented by William and Friedrich Siemens, German-born scientists living in England. It is also called the Siemens-Martin furnace.
1876. English metallurgists Sidney and Percy Gilchrist use a basic lining for the open-hearth furnace to make possible the smelting of high-phosphorus pig iron.
1883. English metallurgist Robert Hadfield discovers tough, durable manganese steel.
1886. Charles Hall in the United States and Paul Héroult in France independently develop the modern electrolytic process of extracting aluminum.
1896. Swiss physicist Charles Gaullaume invents invar, an iron-nickel alloy, notable because it hardly expands when heated.
1899. Paul Héroult begins making steel in an electric-arc furnace.
1900. Frederick Taylor in the United States introduces high-speed cutting tools made from tungsten-chromium steel.
1909. Alfred Wilm in Germany discovers the phenomenon of ageing in aluminum alloys, in which they harden slowly after heat treatment.
1913. Harry Brearley in Britain discovers that adding chromium to steel makes it stainless. The Krupp company in Germany subsequently introduce a steel containing 18 parts chromium and 8 parts nickel — the so-called 18/8 stainless steel.
1949. The basic-oxygen process of steelmaking was developed in Austria. It is also known as the L-D process after the towns of Linz and Donawitz where it was developed.
1950. Continuous casting of steel begins on a large scale.

Books to read

The Picture Book of Metals by Anita Brooks (Harper & Row, 1972)
Gold and Other Precious Metals by Charles Coombs (William Morrow, 1981)
Metals: Background Information by Don Radford (Raintree Books, 1977)
The Story of Metals (International Book Center)
Metals by Raymond A. Wohlrabe (Lippincott, 1964)

Further information

You can find out a lot more about metals by writing to the following associations and companies and asking them to send you copies of their educational and promotional literature.

The Aluminum Association
818 Connecticut Avenue, NW
Washington, D.C. 20006

American Iron and Steel Institute
Communications and Educational Services Dept.
1000 16th Street, NW
Washington, D.C. 20036

Institute of Scrap Iron and Steel, Inc.
1627 K Street, NW
Washington, D.C. 20006

The Copper Development Association
405 Lexington Avenue, 57th Floor
New York, NY 10017

The Malayan Tin Bureau
2000 K Street, NW
Washington, D.C. 20006

The Silver Institute
1001 Connecticut Ave., NW Suite 1138
Washington, D.C. 20036

The Zinc Institute
292 Madison Avenue
New York, New York 10017

The American Society for Metals
Metals Park, Ohio 44073

United States Steel Corporation
600 Grant Street
Pittsburgh, Pennsylvania 15203

Reynolds Aluminum
Richmond, Virginia 23261

Aluminum Co. of America
1501 Alcoa Building
Pittsburgh, Pennsylvania 15219

Kaiser Aluminum
300 Lakeside Drive
Oakland, California 94643

Metal superlatives

Lightest metal: Lithium has a density of 0·53 grams per cubic centimetre – about half the density of water.
Heaviest metal: Osmium has a density of 22·5 grams per cubic centimetre – twice as heavy as lead.
Metal with lowest melting point: Mercury has a melting point of −38·9°C. Of the metals solid at room temperature, caesium has the lowest melting point, 28·6°C.
Metal with highest melting point: Tungsten has a melting point of 3380°C.
Commonest metal: Aluminium is the commonest in the Earth's crust, of which it comprises about 8 per cent. Iron (about 5 per cent of the crust) is probably the commonest in the Earth as a whole if, as seems likely, it makes up most of the molten core of the Earth.
Rarest metal is astatine. The Earth's crust contains at any time only about one-third of a gram of astatine, which is fleetingly formed during the radioactive decay of uranium.
Most ductile metal is gold. One kilogram of gold can be drawn out into over 2,000 kilometres of very fine wire.
Most malleable metal is gold. One kilogram of gold can be beaten into a very thin sheet 1,000 square metres in area.
Most toxic metal is plutonium. Much less than one-millionth of a gram, if swallowed or inhaled, will cause cancer. Plutonium remains deadly for tens of thousands of years.

Below: The periodic table is shown here as it relates to metals. The elements 57-71 are the rare earth elements such as lanthanum, and elements 89-103, which include uranium, are radioactive. The inert gases group, such as helium, have been left off the diagram. The names of the elements shown, and their symbols, are listed below.

Aluminium (Al)
Antimony (Sb)
Arsenic (As)
Astatine (At)
Barium (Ba)
Beryllium (Be)
Bismuth (Bi)
Boron (B)
Bromine (Br)
Cadmium (Cd)
Calcium (Ca)
Carbon (C)
Caesium (Cs)
Chlorine (Cl)
Chromium (Cr)
Cobalt (Co)
Copper (Cu)
Fluorine (F)
Francium (Fr)
Gallium (Ga)
Germanium (Ge)
Gold (Au)
Hafnium (Hf)
Hydrogen (H)
Indium (In)
Iodine (I)
Iridium (Ir)
Iron (Fe)
Lead (Pb)
Lithium (Li)
Magnesium (Mg)
Manganese (Mn)
Mercury (Hg)
Molybdenum (Mo)
Nickel (Ni)
Niobium (Nb)
Nitrogen (N)
Osmium (Os)
Oxygen (O)
Palladium (Pd)
Phosphorus (P)
Platinum (Pt)
Polonium (Po)
Potassium (K)
Radium (Ra)
Rhenium (Re)
Rhodium (Rh)
Rubidium (Rb)
Ruthenium (Ru)
Scandium (Sc)
Selenium (Se)
Silicon (Si)
Silver (Ag)
Sodium (Na)
Strontium (Sr)
Sulphur (S)
Tantalum (Ta)
Technetium (Tc)
Tellurium (Te)
Thallium (Tl)
Tin (Sn)
Titanium (Ti)
Tungsten (W)
Vanadium (V)
Yttrium (Y)
Zinc (Zn)
Zirconium (Zr)

Acknowledgements

Artists
Keith Duran, John Flynn, Tony Gibbons, and Brian Watson by courtesy of Linden Artists.

Photographs
Key: T (top); B (bottom); R (right)
Anglo-American Corporation of South Africa Limited: 22
Aspect Picture Library: 41T
Paul Brierley: 13, 37L
British Aerospace: 42T
British Leyland: 17T
British Steel Corporation: 26, 30, 31, 35T
City of Bristol Museum and Art Gallery: 10
Central Office of Information/Royal Mint: 35B
Cooper-Bridgeman Library: 32
David Cripp/Jacqueline Mina: 40
Daily Telegraph Colour Library: 41B
Douglas Dickens: 23B
Robert Harding Picture Library: 11, 23T
Alfred Herbert Ltd: 38
Angelo Hornak: 15
Institute of Oceanographic Sciences: 45
Robin Kerrod: 16, 37R, 42B, 43C B
The Mining Journal Ltd: 44
Rex Features: 27
Spectrum Colour Library: 17B
Tony Stone Associates: front cover
John Topham Picture Library: 2-3, 33
UBE Chemical Industries: 29
UKAEA: 19, 43T
Janine Wiedel: 45
ZEFA: 9

Periodic table of the elements

Atomic number — 79
Symbol of element — Au
Atomic weight — 196·97

Metals, metalloids and non-metals

Lighter metals ← Heavier metals →

												5	6	7	8	9
H												B	C	N	O	F
												10·81	12·01	14·01	16·00	19·00
3	4											13	14	15	16	17
Li	Be											Al	Si	P	S	Cl
6·94	9·01											26·98	28·09	30·97	32·06	35·45
11	12															
Na	Mg															
22·99	24·31															
19	20	21	22	23	24	25	26	27	28	29	30	31	32	33	34	35
K	Ca	Sc	Ti	V	Cr	Mn	Fe	Co	Ni	Cu	Zn	Ga	Ge	As	Se	Br
39·10	40·08	44·96	47·90	50·94	51·99	54·94	55·85	58·93	58·71	63·54	65·37	69·72	72·59	74·92	78·96	79·91
37	38	39	40	41	42	43	44	45	46	47	48	49	50	51	52	53
Rb	Sr	Y	Zr	Nb	Mo	Tc	Ru	Rh	Pd	Ag	Cd	In	Sn	Sb	Te	I
85·47	87·62	88·91	91·22	92·91	95·94	(99)	101·07	102·91	106·4	107·87	112·40	114·82	118·69	121·75	127·60	126·90
55	56	elements 57 to 71	72	73	74	75	76	77	78	79	80	81	82	83	84	85
Cs	Ba		Hf	Ta	W	Re	Os	Ir	Pt	Au	Hg	Tl	Pb	Bi	Po	At
132·91	137·34		178·49	180·95	183·85	186·2	190·2	192·2	195·09	196·97	200·59	204·37	207·19	208·98	(210)	(210)
87	88	elements 89 to 103														
Fr	Ra															
(223)	(226)															

47

Index

Numbers in *italics* refer to illustrations

Actinides, 44
Age-hardening, 14, 44
Airframe testing, *18, 19*
Alchemists, 46
Alkali metals, 44
Alloy, 6, 14, *14*
　steels, 7, 15
Aluminium, *4,* 6, 7, *7,* 9, 11, 20, 29, *43,* 44, 46
　refining, 9
Amalgam, 44
Annealing, 34, 44
Anode, 28
Anodizing, 44
Antarctica, *17*
Antimony, 44
Arsenic, *4*
Astatine, 47
Atoms, *4,* 15

Babbit metal, 44, 46
Basic-oxygen furnace, *24,* 30, 46
Bauxite, 9
Beryllium, 44
Bessemer, Henry, 11, 46
Billets, 25
Bingham Canyon, 23, *23*
Bismuth, 44
Blacksmith, *32*
Blast furnace, *24, 26, 26,* 27
Blasting, *22,* 23
Blooms, 25
Brass, *8, 14,* 36
Brazing, 36
Brittleness, 5
Bronze, 6, 7, *8,* 11, *14,* 41
　casting, *10,* 32

Cadmium, 44
Calipers, *19*
Carbon, 14, 15, 30
Cars, metallic, 7
Cast iron, *4,* 5, *6*
Casting, 25, *31,* 32, *32*
Cathode, 28
Cermet, 44
Chemical elements, 4
Chinese ironmaking, 11, 46
Chrome, 20
Chromium, *4,* 44
Cobalt, *20,* 44
Coke, 26
Compression, 16, *16*
Concrete, 6
Copper, *4, 4, 8,* 9, *10, 13,* 14, 20, *20,* 29, 44
Copperbelt, 9
Corrosion, 16, *16*
Cort, Henry, 46
Crystals, *43, 45*
　lattice, 13, 15
　structure, *13*
Cupronickel, *14,* 44
Cutting, 38, *39*
Cyanide process, 28

Darby, Abraham, 46,
Davy, Humphry, 28, 46
Dendrite, 13, *13*
Destructive testing, 18
Downs cell, *28*
Drawing, *34,* 35
Dredgers, 23, *23*
Drilling, 39, *39*
Ductile strength, 5, 44
Duralumin, 14, *14,* 44

Earth's crust, *21*
Elastic limit, 16, 44
Electric-arc
　furnace, *24, 30,* 31
　welding, 37
Electrolysis, 28, *28, 29,* 31, 44
Electron, 4
　beam welding, *43*
　microscope, *12*
Electroplating, 17
Embossing, 41, *41*
Etching, 12, *12,* 41
Explosive forming, 34

Fatigue, metal, 16
Feeler gauge, *19*
Fibreglass, 43
Flotation, 24, *44*
Fool's gold, 9
Forge, 25, *32, 33*

Galvanizing, 7, 12, 17
Gangue, 24, 44
Gases, furnace, 27
Germanium, 44
Gilding, 41
Gold, 20, *20,* 22, 23, *40,* 46
Grain structure, 12, *12*
Great Britain, 10
Gunmetal, 15, 44

Hafnium, 44
Hall-Héroult process, 11, 29
Hallmarking, *41*
Hardness, 18
Heat treatment, 15, 44
Hooke's law, 44
Hot-blast stoves, 27
Hydraulic mining, 23

Impact extrusion, 34, *34*
Ingots, 25, *33*
Injection moulding, 33
Iron, 6, *6,* 8, 9, *13,* 20, *41*
　Age, 11
　cast, *4,* 5, *6*
　corrosion, *16*
　pig, 27, 30
　reserves, 8
　smelting, 26
　steel and, 24-25
　wrought, 11
Izod test, 18

Jewellery, 7, *10, 40*

Laser welding, 37
Lathe, *38,* 39

Lattice, crystal, 13, *13,* 15
Leaching, 29
Lead, *20,* 27, *30,* 44
Lithium, 4, 44, 46
Lost-wax process, *10*

Machine tools, 38
Magma, 20
Malleability, 5, 32, 44
Manganese, *13,* 20, *20*
　nodules, *42,* 44
　steel, 5
Measuring instruments, *19*
Mercury, *4, 4, 20, 45,* 46
Metallurgy, 5, 11, 25
Metals,
　civilization and, *10-11*
　corrosion and, 16
　crystals/grains, 12-13, *45*
　extraction, 24, 26
　fatigue, 16
　joining/cutting, 36-37
　mining and, 22-23
　properties, 4-6
　recycling, *43, 43*
　refining, 30-31
　reserves, 42
　shaping, 32-35
　sources, 20-21
　strength, 15
　stresses and, 16
　testing/measuring, 18-19
　uses, 6-7
　See also individual metals
Metalworking, 38-41
Micrometer, *19*
Mild steel, *6,* 14, 45
Milling, 39, *39*
Mineral dressing, 2, 45
Mining, 22-23
Molybdenum, 20, 45
Mould, 32, *32*

New Orleans, *41*
Nickel, *20, 27,* 45
Non-destructive testing, 18
Non-metals, 4
Nuclear submarine, 7

Open-hearth furnace, *24,* 30
Opencast mining, 23, *23*
Ores,
　origins, 20
　smelting, 26-27
Osmiridium, 15
Osmium, 45, 46
Oxides, 20
Oxyacetylene, 36, *36*

Paint, 17, *17*
Periodic table, *47*
Pig iron, 27, 30
Placer deposits, 20, 23
Platinum, 6, *20, 40,* 45
Plutonium, 47
Powder metallurgy, 45
Pressing, 34, *35*
Process metallurgy, 25
Propeller, ship's, *33*

Queen Mary, 37
Quenching, 11, 15, 45

Radium, 45
Rare earths, 45
Reaming, 39
Recycling, *43, 43*
Refining, 9, 24, 30-31
Refractory materials, 45
Resistance welding, 37
Riveting, 36
Rockets, *42*
Rolling, *33,* 34
Roughing mill, *25*
Rust, 16, *16*

Salt solution, 17, 28
Screws, *39*
Shaping metal, 32-35
Shear forces, 16, *16*
Siemens-Martin furnace, 46
Silver, 20, *28,* 40, *41,* 45
Sinter, 24
Slag, 26
Smelting, 24, 26-27
Sodium, *4, 28, 28,* 45
Soldering, 36, *37,* 45
Space age, *42, 43*
Spinning, 34
Spraying, *17*
Stamping, 34, *35*
Steel, 4, *5,* 6, 7, 15, *24-25,* 30
　mild, *6,* 14, 45
　stainless, 15, 46
　tungsten, 15
Surgical aids, 7
Stresses 16, *16*
Suspension bridge, *6,* 7

Tempering, 15, 45
Tensile test, 18
Tension, 16, *16*
Test rig, *18*
Thermometer, *4*
Tin, *20,* 45
　plate, 7
Titanium, 7, 45
Tornado, 42
Transition metals, 45
Tungsten, 20, 45, 46
　carbide, 7
　steel, 15
Tutankhamun, 11

Ultrasonic testing, 18, *19*
Uranium, 6, 7, *13,* 20, 45

'Welcome Stranger', 20
Welding, 36, *36, 43*
Wilm, Alfred, 46
Wire, 7
　drawing, *34,* 35
Wood's metal, 45
Wrought iron, 11

X-rays, 13, 18

Zinc, *5,* 20, 27, 45
Zirconium, 45

PROPERTY OF WAYNE COUNTY
INTERMEDIATE SCHOOL DISTRICT
CHAPTER 2, P.L. 97-35

669
KER   Kerrod, Robin

       Metals

DATE DUE	BORROWER'S NAME	ROOM NUMBER
FEB 2 6	LaCoure	301
MAR 1 1	LaCoure	301
MAR 2 1	M. Hendricks	301
APR 3 0	LaCoure	301
MAY 0 8	Joe Wimson	301
DE 1 03	Joshua Rainer	304

GESU SCHOOL LIBRARY
DETROIT, MICH. 48221

DEMCO